So You Think Your Kid's Got Talent!

by

Jessica Elliott

Edited by Nicole D'Entremont Novel Treasure

ISBN: 9781791523794
Imprint: Independently published

Dedicated to my very own
Tiny Superstars!

Louise Elliott-George- Dance with the angels in
heaven & be the brightest spotlight in the sky!
I Love you and always will.

Storm-Aurora George- You danced into
my life & make me smile every single day!
I am so proud of you & love you dearly.

Mummy x

Contents

"All I got is dreams. Nobody else can see, nobody else but me."
- Jay Z

INTRODUCTION
MUM, I WANNA BE FAMOUS!

That sentence either fills you with excitement or absolute dread! I will be frank, in today's world it is quite possible to achieve the kind of fame and money they desire with little or no talent with the help of reality TV shows catapulting them to new heights. However, I'm sure you'll agree that they have a bigger shot at an actual career with longevity by carving out a career that capitalises on their talent and passions. This book contains 28 years of knowledge. From starting out at dance classes, attending stage school, experiencing auditions, becoming a dance teacher and performance coach, to setting up my own dance academies and talent agency. I am baring all to save you from making the same mistakes that parents make time after time, all in the search for stardom for their very own superstar!

Whose Dream is it Anyway?

Before we go any further, there is one thing I'd like you to remember: The kids that are the most successful are kids who want to work, have big dreams and work hard to achieve them. The dream must be theirs and not yours! It's not cool to live your dreams of Hollywood through your child or 'force them' to do this because it's what you want. The decision needs to be 100% theirs.

You may be thinking, 'but a four-year-old doesn't know what they want.' Well, I beg to differ. Here are some clues:

- They cry every single time you take them to dance class

- You've already tried auditioning, and they clammed up every single time
- They are overly shy or introverted,

They tell you they don't want to do it
You'll probably find those Hollywood dreams are yours and not theirs.

As a parent, you need to be a support system to their dreams, not them supporting yours! Now, that may sting your pride a little. But in the long run, if you push them into an industry or environment they are not interested in, you will end up with a very unhappy and somewhat disconnected child who does things just to please you as opposed to being happy too. Not cool!

My Steps to the Spotlight

From the moment I could talk, I only ever wanted to become two things, a dancer and a dentist (Strange, I know!). I actually did end up going to dental school as I had a dream of owning both a dental practice and a dance studio on the same premises, but I quit dental school (That's another book in itself). My earliest memories were at a dance school. I spent every weekend dancing from as long as I can remember. I absolutely loved it, and for me, I lived for the weekends. I looked forward to learning new routines, seeing my dance friends, and working towards the next show or set of dance exams. It truly was my passion! Not to mention how I felt on the stage! .

However, I was never the kid who got all the main parts in the plays or solos. Deep down inside, I knew that I was a fantastic performer. My grandmother had instilled in me that nobody was better than me, a statement I live my life by till this very day. But for some reason, growing up, it was always the same people getting the star roles. I remember one show, in particular, I sang three words out of place just to create a little solo for myself! I was chuffed, even though it was only three little words. But, my voice was heard.

For a brief time, my family moved to New York due to my Dad's work commitments. I attended the Perfection Dance Centre in New York when I was about nine. The Principal of the dance school further instilled in me that I was an amazing dancer with loads of potential and had the power to achieve anything. I remember having to answer to my name in the register with "My name is Jessica, and I am somebody." Showtime came around, yet still no solos or main parts though!

Unbeknownst to me, these dance schools shaped the rest of my life. At that time, I made a promise to myself to set up my own dance school. When I was an adult, I was going to give everyone equal opportunities. 11 years after writing that in my little lockable diary, designing logos and the uniform that everyone would wear, that's exactly what I did. While studying for my degree, I found a dance teacher training course that I could do while studying (I actually now lecture on that very same qualification myself.) After months of hard work, I qualified to become a dance teacher and off I went with £200 and a dream to start a dance business while at university! My Mum always said to me, "You'll get your chance one day!" And I sure did, just not in the way I thought it would come.

In 2007, I started my dance school with eight kids (two of which I was related to) in a church hall in South London in the UK. It was only eight kids, but none of that mattered. I had people to teach! It didn't take long before I filled the classes and had over 70 children attending on a weekly basis. Within 3 months, I was able to produce my own show, and guess what? Everyone had a chance to perform and stand in the front row if they wanted to. 200 people bought tickets and it was a great feeling. I went on to launch a second school in another part of London before franchising it, being featured in the world's biggest publications, being invited to interview the Prime Minister, and winning over 10 business awards including young entrepreneur of the year twice!

Mums are always right! I got my time to shine. I'd been running the school for about four years when we did a show, and I was approached by a talent scout about one of my students auditioning for a lead role in a West End show in London. I had zero clue about how the industry worked from a business perspective, but I made sure to find out and set up my own talent agency. That boy went on to be my first client and landed the role of Simba in the Lion King in London's West End! Boom! Success! So I began taking on my very first clients aged between four and eleven. I worked my socks off to help nurture these amazing kids, be a fountain of knowledge and a support system for their parents. The agency has gone on to be a massive success.

I never take on large amounts of clients and always run the agency on my own terms and with love! My students have been featured in worldwide ad campaigns, International stages, T.V. shows, and more while remaining grounded and humble. They are among the hardest working people I know but have so much fun! And that's exactly how it should be! I have carved out a niche job for myself which I absolutely love and enjoy. I get to help young people realise their dreams, visit sets and stages worldwide, and support parents through the process of their child getting to and being in the spotlight! Is life easy? No! But is everyday worth it? YES! I work with the most awesome people. It is quite ironic that as a child, I dreamt of being a star, but now, I don't think I could have any greater satisfaction than seeing my young clients achieve their dreams, even if I was performing myself.

So, why this book? Well, I get a ton of parents who simply don't know what to do to support their child in the process of finding work in the entertainment industry. I constantly get asked, "how do you get an agent?" "What about school?" And a ton of other questions, so I thought it's only right that I put down my knowledge in a book which will answer everything you will ever need to know about your child working in the entertainment industry. I don't want to hear about how parents have been 'ripped off' or paid out thousands of dollars because so-called agents have taken advantage of their dreams and often exploited their vulnerability. It is my mission to finally arm parents with the knowledge they need to help their child achieve their dreams while keeping them safe, happy, and growing in all aspects of life. So, what are we waiting for? Let's hit the stage…

"All I want to do is be on stage, a performer needs to perform."
- David Hasselhoff

CHAPTER 1

LIGHTS, CAMERA, ACTION!

TV, Theatre, Film, or Fashion

There are a ton of different jobs available. It is helpful to know what type of jobs your child wants to go for. You see, working in the fashion industry such as catwalk or print modelling is very different to working in TV. Maybe your child wants to do it all at first, and that's fine, but I'm sure it will not be long before they work out exactly what they prefer. Some would say you shouldn't be choosy when starting out, but I totally disagree. Entertainment is highly competitive, and your child will do so much better working in a field they are truly passionate about and actually good at. In this chapter, we will explore the different types of jobs it's possible to have.

The Bright Lights of Broadway

There are a variety of children's roles available in theatre. Over the years, I have managed children who appear night in and night out in London's West End for Disney, The Royal Shakespeare Company, and the Royal Opera House to name a few. While this looks glamorous, the reality is theatre jobs are hard work. Depending on the size of the role, rehearsals are often intense, and children are expected to take quick direction. In some shows, they may be the only kid in the cast. For most Broadway and West End shows, if it's a lead role, children work in pairs or a group of three or four so that they do not exceed the legal number of hours they can work and go to school. It also helps them avoid burnout. Partners also stand in if a child is sick and unable to perform.

You will find that even if your child does three shows a week, you may have to be at the theatre five or six times a week at a minimum. If the theatre put on eight shows a week, the days your child is not performing your child will have to be a standby. Once they have been cast in a show, there may also be the need to attend extra rehearsals. The length of a contract is generally six months, and quite often if things haven't changed too much the production team may choose to renew, but you should not take this as a given right!

Your child will be expected to sing, dance, act, and perform to a high standard night after night! Kids with previous musical theatre training are often favoured, show after show. Bare in mind that shows often finish at 10 pm and sometimes your child will have to stay until curtain call (the bow at the end). They are then expected to go to school the following day on time. For your child to work in theatre, you'll both need to be super dedicated and willing to get used to late nights and early mornings. The financial rewards are not the biggest, so you'll have to be in it for the love of the show. The experience and exposure are something money can't buy. It is also great fun and parents and kids often make lifetime friendships.

TOP 5 TIPS FOR WEST END/BROADWAY MUMS

1. Get organised - Have your child's performance schedule printed out and put on the fridge. Especially if you have other children, it's important you look at all dates in your diary early on so you can get help with picking up and dropping off your child to the theatre, should there be date clashes with other important appointments.
2. Don't be afraid to ask for help - Heading into the city three, four, or sometimes five times a week can be exhausting. Share the responsibility amongst family and friends and if things are becoming too much talk to your agent, ask for help. Do not run yourself into the ground when there may be a simple solution that can help make life easier.
3. Plan for when you will see the show - Find out the ticket policy and book that in your diary. Family and friends are often keen to see your child in action too. Send out a timetable of your child's performances and a link for them to book tickets, so they do not come to you. Also, be sure to tell them that while it should be ok, the schedule can change at the last hour so you can not 100% guarantee. Try to space out the number of people your child knows in the audience so that someone can be watching them all the time. Don't book tickets in the front row or somewhere your child will see you. It can be overwhelming and hugely off-putting for them. Especially, if it's their very first show. Think about whether you will tell your child that someone they know is watching them. If you think it will add pressure or make them nervous, do not tell them.
4. Get to know the other parents of the children in the show - It's a much nicer experience if you do this with people who understand what you are going through and more often than not parents from the same show become a great support to each other.
5. Enjoy it - This will not last forever, enjoy every minute of the roller coaster because one day, when the contract comes to an end you won't be doing it anymore and you will probably miss it!

Strike a Pose

Everyone you meet tells you to get your child into modelling, they are a dab hand at selfie-taking, and they are only three years old. Totally gifted. So, you want to get them into fashion modelling. Here's the thing. To survive in the very competitive fashion world and actually get jobs, your child will need to have more than just a pretty face.

You see, even the prettiest child in the world may not be a great model. Kids must be able to turn on the charm on tap and pose in a way that doesn't appear forced or awkward and make movements that really represent a brand. I believe that most child models have an innate natural ability to work the camera and bring out the best in any brand. You see, you have to remember your child will be representing a brand, not themselves. So, while that photoshoot you did with them on your iPhone on the beach during your last family holiday was great; It may not translate when they step in front of the camera as they are completely different skills.

The world of fashion is very diverse, so different personality types will suit different shoots depending on the clothes, product, or brand. This is fantastic as it allows a child to be themselves, which is so effective and really shows in the end result. It also means that a child doesn't necessarily need to be overly extroverted to succeed in child modelling as long as they are able to use their character to their advantage, perhaps by exaggerating certain moods or tendencies and are confident within themselves.

Shoots are often carried out over one or two days, and there can be multiple clothing changes. It can often be quite a busy environment. Days are long and can be tiring, but there is no better feeling than your child seeing their photo on a bus or billboard or even in a magazine. Like most jobs in this industry, your child will need to take direction well and be comfortable and happy having their photo taken multiple times and following instructions which aren't always 'be happy and smile.'

Catwalk shows are great fun and often long days, but also a great way for kids to express their personality. Catwalk modelling is not as easy as it looks. Children will often have to hit certain points on the catwalk at specific times and learn the skill of showing the audience the clothes they are wearing while walking or sometimes dancing. Quite often now, fashion week features more and more child models, as designers opt to showcase their youth collections. Shopping centres and malls also often have kids fashion shows to attract customers to their stores. Don't be fooled by fancy labels, top-end designers often do not pay children the kind of fees you would expect, but generally, the rate of pay is fair.

One of my 13-year-old clients has modelled for the likes of Stella McCartney, been featured in Vogue Paris and worked with International sports brands.... Here's a young fashion model's advice for doing well on a fashion shoot!

TOP 5 TIPS FOR A CHILD MODEL
(Share this with your kids)

1. It's really exciting but try to go to bed early the night before because shoots are long days.
2. Always listen to the Director and try to follow instructions the first time on how they want you to walk or pose.
3. Take a book or your IPad to use during the times when you are not rehearsing or shooting. Sometimes, there is a lot of waiting around.
4. Try to be sociable and chat with everyone on set but not when you are supposed to be working.
5. Send a 'thank you for having me' note after the shoot and let them know you are thankful for the opportunity and enjoyed it!

Top of the Box

Child actors are often, without doubt, the most loved members of any TV or film cast. Okay, and the animals if there are any. Whoever said never work with kids or animals just didn't know what they were talking about! TV and films can be amazing for any child to be a part of. It is important that you drop any visions you have of Hollywood glamour, as TV and film are often a far cry from that but, it is a ton of fun!

TV and film jobs are suited to kids who have great attention to detail and who have great concentration. Children must have good listening skills and be able to take direction and put feedback into practice immediately. Working in TV and film requires an immense amount of patience and a genuine love for the job because scenes often need to be shot over and over again from different angles. Now that everything is screened in HD, the ability to stay focused and consistent is also a must because the camera picks up even the slightest movement or inconsistency.

Scenes are not often filmed in sequence, which means that they could be filming the end of an episode or film the first day they step onto a set. In some ways, being on a TV show takes the magic out of watching television slightly because you learn all the secrets of how everything is done. This sector of the industry is probably the most diverse. Your child doesn't need to have a certain look or be traditionally 'pretty.' It's about whether their face and personality fit the character needed in the production.

In terms of time commitment, this is stated at the beginning of the project, but from experience, it can have a tendency to take more time perhaps due to losing time because of weather conditions or cast illness. Depending on the role, your child may be needed on set for a day or need to be there for a period of weeks or months for a show with various episodes or a feature film. Do not be at all surprised if your child has all of three lines in a show or film, but spent two weeks on set. Filming can be a long process. It's important to get the small detail right. So, it can be time-consuming, but I'm sure when you watch your little (or big) star on that screen the hard work and the dropping off and picking up from rehearsals and sets will be worth it.

If your child is cast in a TV show, their filming schedule will depend on the involvement of their character at the time. Similarly to theatre jobs, holidays will be prohibited during filming in order for the production team to keep to a strict filming schedule.

Many children start their career in television as supporting artists (SA). An SA used to be referred to as an extra. This means that they do not have lines, or if they do, they say less than a sentence but help to set the scene. Popular supporting actor roles for kids are making up a class in a classroom scene or playing on a playground. Being an SA often involves the same time commitment as those with lead roles, but it is a fantastic introduction to life on set and really allows children to 'learn the ropes' and in fact test it out and see if it is something they actually even want to do.

In terms of payment, budgets vary from job to job so it's actually hard to advise on exactly what your child will earn. It could be from hundreds to thousands. Pay is usually a daily rate, but for a serial drama or sometimes a film, a fixed fee may be negotiated.

Commercials

Some of the clients that I have represented in the past and, in fact, still do to this day only work on TV commercials. They love it, and one of the great things about it is that they are usually one-day shoots and no longer than three. Commercials are a fantastic entry into the entertainment industry. Great for building confidence, sometimes, kids may even have to learn short scripts too, but the greatest thing of all is there is so much experience to be gained in taking direction. More often than not, commercials see children carrying out actions. The director will work with those children to direct them on how they should move and exactly what to do. It's a fab chance for your child to practice taking direction in preparation for entering the world of TV and film. Your child doesn't need to have any previous acting experience to begin working on commercials, and you will probably start off taking them to commercial castings and auditions when they first start out, especially if you sign to a talent agency. Success relies on their ability to take direction as well as their own personality being a 'great fit' for the brand.

In terms of financial reward, commercials are often the highest earners! This is because, on top of the child's daily rate, they are paid what is called a 'buy out fee.' This fee is paid to a child if they are featured in the advert. In the contract, it will state exactly what the buyout fee covers, but essentially, it is a fee to use footage of your child in certain forms, e.g., TV, and web content and territories in the UK or worldwide. This fee is nearly always negotiable and often runs into thousands of pounds per commercial.

You've Got a Great Voice for Radio

Remember, commercials are not always TV commercials. Companies still advertise on the radio and sometimes want a child's voice at the centre of the campaign. Likewise, children's film or TV shows often require a child's voice. Children can be successful in voiceover work and earn themselves a small fortune in the process depending on the job.

Probably the most famous child for doing this is Harley Bird. Now, that name may not mean anything to you, but if you have a preschooler, you will be very familiar with her voice as she has been the voice of Peppa Pig for ten years. Her voice features in all episodes, merchandise, talking books, and even a feature film. Peppa Pig is worth an estimated 141 million pounds, and Harley is the star of the show! Voice-Over work is few and far between, but a great opportunity if your child gets to do it.

I think it's perfect for extremely talented direction focused children who do not necessarily seek the limelight, as it is important to remember that if you are the voice of something, no one will actually see their faces most of the time. In fact, maybe only for promotional purposes.

Pack That Suitcase

Locations for projects in the entertainment industry can be all over the world. I know what you are thinking... I pray they get a job in The Maldives for six months! Heavenly right?! Yeah, I'd love that too... anyway, I digress. The point is, some jobs will mean that your child has to travel at times. Domestically and internationally. As a parent, you will need to think about if both you and your child are ready for that or not. It may mean being without you and travelling with a licensed chaperone for prolonged periods of time. It will depend on the nature of the job. They may travel with the rest of the cast, or on occasion, you will need to travel with them. You will need to think about how this will affect work commitments.

Travel is a massive commitment, so you will meet your child's chaperones and get the opportunity to learn more about them before-hand. Chaperones who travel with children are usually very experienced. Before your child travels, you should feel assured that they will be looked after. Ask your agent to see a copy of any security checks that have been done on the chaperone and a copy of their CV too. You can ask to speak to the parent of a child who has been looked after by this chaperone before. That helps to ease stress. Your child will need to learn the basics of looking after themselves too. Often parents think their child will not cope with this, but if your child does get the chance to tour, most find that it's an incredible experience and one they'll never forget.

The financial rewards and the duration of the contract depend on the nature of the job, but aside from any fees, children are paid a daily sum of money called per diems. This is to cover the daily cost of meals and other small expenses. It is usually managed by whoever is looking after the child's well-being and responsible for their daily care.

5 TIPS FOR TRAVELLING KIDS
by an international chaperone

1. Think about the size of the bag you are giving your child. If they are only going away for a week, they do not need two weeks' worth of clothes. Bear in mind; there is a large chance they will be in costume most of the time. While as chaperones, we will always help them but they need to be able to manage the luggage themselves.
2. Do not put sweets and a stash of sugary snacks in your child's bag. You may think you are being kind, but a sugar rush at ten o'clock at night is not what they need.
3. Feel free to check in on how your child is getting on using the process that is set up prior to them joining the cast. Try to refrain from texting and calling your child throughout the day as they are either busy in rehearsals, being tutored, or performing. There is usually a time set aside daily to call home. Phones are sometimes kept by chaperones throughout the day for safekeeping.
4. Don't send your child with anything you would be disappointed about if it were to get lost. I've experienced the loss of designer coats, expensive boots, and watches. Leave valuables and their best clothes at home.
5. Get to know your chaperone. They are there to help you as well as your child. There are kids I chaperoned years ago, and I am still in touch with the children and their families.

"If you can dream it, you can do it!"
- Walt Disney

CHAPTER 2

TALK TO MY AGENT

For your kids to gain quality jobs that will enrich their lives and develop their craft, they will need some form of management. That management could take on many forms. Here, we talk agents, management, and all you need to know about making the right choice for your budding star!

Now, here's the thing. We all want an agent, right? I mean how cool would it be to take us back to our ten-year-old self on the playground, telling our friends that we have an agent! Amazing, huh? But agents are not just there in name only. They have an important role to play in the development of your child.

Do We Really Need an Agent?

An agent's job is not just to call you up and send you to auditions. They hold the responsibility of nurturing your child, helping them to further their career. Good agents take a holistic approach to the representation of your child as well as you and your family. Great agents often become your biggest support system and a sounding board when decisions need to be made, or you need advice about the industry as a whole. A pretty important job I am sure you will agree!

An agent is an advisor to your child and family and will 'check in' with you regularly, having the wellbeing of your child at the centre of all that they do. Agents have gone out there and made the connections, so know where all the jobs are and who to put your child in front of to give them the best chance of getting work. So, does your child really need an agent? Yes, in some form because they need someone to network and promote their wonderful talents on their behalf to ensure they actually get work or at least get sent for castings and auditions. The process will be much easier as you, and your child will be supported. However, it is important to remember that there are no guarantees.

The Perfect Match

What I have described is exactly how an agent should be and what their role in your child's career should look like. I know my clients personally and their families; sometimes, extended family members and most definitely siblings. This is truly important for the pastoral role of an agent as you know when things are happening in the family and can advise on how to manage siblings and help with logistics or auditions, castings and getting the child to and from work. If you do not know the dynamics of a family, it is impossible to give sound, helpful advice. Unfortunately, this is not the case for every agent. So, if taking on an agent is something you want to do it is important you find the right one for your child! Don't worry, I've got you, and I'll tell you exactly what to look for and how to find one.

These days we are really lucky! We have the whole world in the palm of our hand. A blessing and curse (some may say), but in this case, you have access to every agent's online platform; from their website to all their social media accounts. Take a look. See what you find. Choosing an agent is a personal choice go through some websites and see what's out there in your area, what they are offering, and what you are drawn to. Don't just focus on their credits and what their clients have achieved.

Of course, that's a major part of it, but also look at their values, what they say about talent development, and really get a feel for the type of organisation it is.

If you have friends or family who already have agents be sure to ask them. Recommendations are great when finding an agent, so ask around and see whose name keeps coming up. This is a big decision, so you want to get it right. Of course, there may be cases where you have to actually try a few before you get the right fit just like most things in life, but if you put in some research from the beginning, you will find you will make a successful choice. As much as an agent chooses your child, you most definitely choose an agent, and with new agencies popping up all the time, you'll see that there are plenty of choices.

In your search, you will find agencies of various sizes. I've seen agencies with hundreds of kids on their books, and I've seen others with five! That's another decision you will need to make. Do you go big or small? In fact, it's a question I am asked all the time! There are pros and cons to both.

A small agency represents a family environment with a more personal approach and the ability for agents to personally track and follow children's progress and offer support to them and their families. While large agencies can still offer support, my thoughts are the larger the agency, the less personal touch. That does not mean they are not good. Some of them are, just depends on the type of service you prefer. In larger agencies, sometimes, you can experience something called internal competition where they have taken on so many kids that look quite similar, of the same age bracket, and skill set that when jobs come up, there are a ton of kids from the same agency going for the same casting. That means your child may not even get an audition as they may only take one or two of the children that have been suggested to them.

An important thing to consider when choosing your agent is whether you want your child to have sole representation or not. Sole representation would mean that they can only get jobs from that one agent. You would not be able to source jobs yourself or from other agents and you would not be able to attend open auditions without your agent's permission. Now, this is not always a bad thing, if you are signing up with a top agent with a great track record, they may have all of the contacts needed to get your child the type of auditions for jobs they truly desire.

As a general rule, I would be against signing with a sole agent if they are new or not well established, as it takes time to build momentum and network contacts. If you are signed to a solc agent, it could hold your child back as your contract would mean you couldn't seek jobs elsewhere. Remember, great agents should be open to all opportunities, not just the ones they have created. If it's going to develop your child's talents and enrich their experiences. Established agents often have trial periods, although they are 'sole representation' agents. You can try each other out before you make a decision.

If you do opt for signing with a sole agent, be sure to make use of the trial period so that you can try each other out for size. Once you have signed with them, you will not be able to accept work found by any other agent, so you should make sure they have the contact and capacity to search for work for you before signing.

Here are five things to look for when choosing an agent.

1. The agent's morals and values (try to speak to current and past clients as well as talking to the agent themselves).
2. Testimonials from parents - especially those parents you know.
3. The size of the agency - how many kids on their books and more importantly, how many kids on their books that look like yours?
4. Their success - do their kids actually get work?
5. Do they charge to join? (more on this later)

Getting a Yes!

Once you have researched the internet, asked friends, and stalked pages on social media, it's time to draw up a shortlist of your top five agencies.

Let's call this your agency hit list. Note them down and pay attention to their joining procedures. Some agencies are invite only, in which case, you cannot apply. They usually seek your child out, more often than not after they have built up a small portfolio of work or through talent scouting at amateur shows or even on the street. Some only open their books twice a year, and others accept submissions all year round.

Be aware of the procedure for all of the agencies you have picked out and follow the process of application. You may be asked to send a video or photos and some other info. Perhaps fill in a form. Do so and await their response. If you get any no's, don't dwell on those. Focus on the ones that say yes! Most good agencies have an interview process where you will have to meet the agent with your child. Your child may even have to learn a script, a song, or demonstrate a talent. There are also sometimes test shots (a mini photo shoot) taken at the interview in order for the agent to assess your child and their talents fairly. If they accept you without meeting you or having an online interview with you, this should ring alarm bells! You wouldn't employ someone to do a very important job without meeting them at least online first. This is no different.

Be aware that this assessment day or interview is a fantastic way to see if you and the agent are a great fit. Are there tons of kids at the audition day and does it feel chaotic? Is there a warm personal approach? These are all things to look out for. Likewise, agents will be looking at how your child interacts the moment you step into the studio. It is possible to prepare your child for an interview or an assessment day; perhaps they have asked you to come with a script prepared or sing a song but remember this should be something that they want to do and ultimately should be fun! They shouldn't feel stressed or pressured. Remember, this should not be your dream! It's all about their enjoyment. It doesn't work if you drag them to an assessment day kicking and screaming and you getting stressed in the process. If they don't want to do it, perhaps they are not ready yet.

Here are the top five things agents look for when signing a new child.

1. The thing I call "the something about factor!" Sometimes, I can't put my finger on it, but there is just something about a kid which makes me instantly know they have something people will like. It's that spark they give off as soon as they enter a room. Their personality, and everything about them.
2. The ability to listen, cooperate, and take direction - remember it's not all about skills. Directors and people in entertainment want to work with delightful well-behaved children who follow instructions.
3. Adult Interaction - remember that on a lot of jobs your child will have to be comfortable in mostly adult environments. Their ability to interact with adults is paramount.
4. Their attention span - As we have already established, set life/ theatre life is a long process at times. It is essential for an agent that they represent kids they feel can cope concentrating for an extended time frame.
5. Their skills – it's not enough to just be beautiful. It's all about what skills they possess, and they don't necessarily have to be performing arts skills. Are they bi-lingual or do they play an instrument? Ride a horse? (P.S.: never lie. I've seen it get a little awkward when parents lie about their kid's talent, only for a French-speaking audition to come up and the kid can't speak a word of French! Ouch!).

Once the agent has met you, they will then decide if you are a good fit for each other. You will also have to decide too. Perhaps you have been to multiple assessment days or interviews. You will receive one of three answers.

1. Yes! We would love to take on your child and represent them in: fill in the blanks (might be just commercials, might be everything, might be TV).

2. Not right now. Be sure to get feedback, but this answer is usually because they feel that your child needs some further training, development, or to build on skills before they can put them forward for jobs. You should stay in touch and go back when they suggest.
3. No thank you. ALWAYS try to get feedback on these responses. The reason may not be what you think it is and it may be something really helpful that your child can do to improve in the future, or it could simply be that they have enough children with a similar look and talents as your child on their books.

Show My Kid the Money!

So, you are now signed to an agent! Now the hard work begins. They have to get your child auditions, and your child has to perform and get the jobs! Before we go any further let's talk cash!

Agent fees vary. There is no set rule or fee. Agent fees should always be charged as a percentage of fees earned by your child. For example, if your child earns £1000 and the agent fee is 20% the agent will take a fee of £200. All money earned by your child will go straight to your agent, who will then take their portion and then pass on the remaining to your child. Fees should be discussed with your agent from the very beginning. Good agents are very transparent about their commission fees and will only make money when your child does.

To begin a career in entertainment, your child will need their own bank account as fees earned by them can only be paid to them. Sometimes, expenses may be paid on top of the fees; this money will be paid directly to you- the parent or guardian, as you are the one who would have paid out for travel and food. Some productions will also reimburse you for your time. This will be indicated at the time of signing the contract for each job.

If your child gets a 'call back' which is when they meet a casting director, and they want to see them again, sometimes a small fee will be paid. You will need to speak to the agent to establish if this would be the case. Your child should also always be paid for wardrobe fittings, script read-throughs, and any rehearsals they attend. Remember, payment varies from job to job, so it is vital that you are clear on payment before signing anything.

Before signing on the dotted line, you will need to establish if there are any other fees associated with joining the agency. Good agents do not charge joining fees, as they are confident in their ability to get your child work and will then earn money from the jobs your child works on. However, there may be an annual fee for a performance database. In the UK, most agents use Spotlight which is an online directory for casting directors. There are others, some of which do not charge fees. Your agent will be able to submit your child for work by using an online paid platform like Spotlight. And to be honest, most of the higher paying commercials and theatre work is advertised on paid online casting sites. You may need to invest in some decent photographs of your child (more on this in a moment), but other than this, there should be no other costs and what you pay should be able to be recouped in the fee of less than one job. Remember, initial costs should be very minimal. Unless of course the agency offers a package of training which can be super helpful in the development of your child.

Scams

Unfortunately, there are some awful people out there who are just in this industry to make money off of children's Hollywood dreams. They make promises that they cannot guarantee they can fulfil because as I said, no agent can guarantee that they can get you a job. They prey on parents and encourage them to spend money on things that they don't need, charge high joining fees, and do not have the development of your child at heart- just their bank balance. This is really sad, and I see a ton of parents getting burnt year after year. Getting sold a dream and a glossy photo shoot. This is not cool! A genuine agent will make money when your child makes money! They will care about the development of your child because your child's success is their success, both financially and in social proof that they are good at what they do!

If you are reading this and feeling slightly sick, don't worry. It happens to the best of us; even my own Mum with me when I was a child. I had big dreams of treading the boards and making it big. Back then, the yellow pages were the biggest source of info. So, I called an agency I found in the yellow pages (yep, I have always been super proactive) and signed myself up. Sent over photos (snail mail, of course) and my Mum paid out a large sum of money. They took me on without meeting me (alarm bells!). They were happy to use family snaps taken in my garden (alarm bells!) and wanted my Mum to pay to have an appointment to come and see them. Again, alarm bells! I'm sure you have guessed by now that I never got one job with them or our money back.

Today, it's a little easier as you can get reviews very easily. There is social media, and there is the Agents Association who list agents that are members of theirs. To gain membership agencies have to undergo a check and pay a fee, that can also be a good resource to assess how legitimate the agency is too, but with all this said scams still happen, please watch out for scammers! Remember the saying, if it seems too good to be true, it probably is!

Are Freebies Ok?

This is a popular question. The answer is 'Yes' and 'No.' Parents often come to me and tell me about these amazing jobs they have sourced, and when I get down to the nitty-gritty of payment, they tell me that the work is unpaid. In nearly all cases, it is not ok for your child to work for free unless they are new to the industry and trying to gain experience! When we, as adults, go to work, we get paid to do so, and it should be the same for your child. Sometimes, companies know full well that parents will be so eager to get their children on stage or screen that they sometimes exploit and do not offer payment. This is not cool, and payment is something a good agent can handle for you if money is something you don't feel comfortable discussing.

With that being said though, there may be a time when 'free work' is appropriate. For example, test shoots and working as a supporting actor/actress are a great way to build up a child's confidence and gives them experience. A test shoot is not used for commercial purposes but is primarily where creatives (photographers, stylists, make-up artists, and models) come together to test an idea. All parties are unpaid including your child if they are the model. Test shoots can be done at the discretion of the agent. Supporting actors are usually given lunch and transport at a minimum but even then, expenses should always be covered and the exact hours and usage of output, for example, where photos and footage will be used needs to be agreed.

Say Cheese!

It is no secret that your child will need some high resolution, quality images to get started in the industry. Your agent should be able to recommend a good photographer. In fact, some agents have a preferred photographer or one they use in-house. This is understandable as they know the industry requirements and how they want them to look to be received well within the industry. Most casting directors will ask for a 'head shot', which is a head and shoulder photo of your child. It is important to remember that this is not a school portrait, but a photo that needs to show the full personality of your child. There is an art to producing good head shots, and some photographers specialise in it.

You most definitely do not need a portfolio that costs thousands of dollars to produce. All of the kids I have ever represented and who have gone on to work around the world just started with one quality headshot and a fun full-length photo. A portfolio is something you can build as you go, not something to pay out for at the start of a child's career. Photos are incredibly important as it is a director's first impression of your child. Kids' head shots need to be updated a lot more regularly when they are younger because their face is constantly changing. They get new teeth, and their features grow and change. In the digital age we now live in, it also might be worth investing in a showreel, especially once your child has a few jobs under their belt. But talk to your agent about this, as most good agents include showreels for clients as part of their representation.

Here are the top Headshot photographer's tips for great headshots.

1. Avoid wearing dark colour or cartoon characters or logos. Plain block colour in bright tones work great. Take two outfit choices.
2. Do not allow hair to fall in front of your child's face.
3. Do not wear makeup unless it's to hide a blemish and it's always best to have it done professionally.
4. Encourage your child to eat and sleep well the night before.
5. Come prepared to the shoot with hair brushes, a snack, water and clothing pre-hung and ironed.

Mumagers and Daddagers

What do Beyonce, Justin Timberlake (NSYNC), Jayden and Willow Smith, and Kim Kardashian all have in common? Well, they have all been/ still are managed by their Mothers or Fathers. This is a question I get asked a lot! Can't we just represent our own kids? And the answer is well yes you can. However, there is much to consider before taking this on.

You will need to have a really good understanding of the industry, and I would suggest already having plenty of contacts to network with. You need to be confident navigating your way around contracts and have the time to invest in looking for work and negotiating deals. The fact is, most parents do not have the time and skill set to manage their own child. In order for it to work successfully, you'll need to be extremely savvy at marketing and PR, and your communication skills need to be on point. Of course, some parents manage their children's multi-million-dollar careers for years and are able to do it successfully. But, here's the thing.... when managing your child, they will always be your baby first and a client second and rightly so. But I question how good this is for your child's career and your relationship as parent and child. In this business, there is plenty of rejection, and as a parent, you are bound to take it personally at some point, which is not helpful for your child in this game. They will need to learn how to be hardened to rejection pretty quickly and only take on positive, constructive feedback. In my experience, parents who manage their own children sometimes take the rejection way too personally.

The role of a parent is the most important job we will ever take on in our lives, and if you are the Mother or Father of a performing child, your responsibilities increase tenfold as you navigate the world of recalls, rejections, and rehearsals. The role of a parent should be to nurture and support your child through this- something that is extremely difficult to do well if you are on the business side of things too. It is very easy to get caught up in the money, the fame, and the potential opportunities which can lead your child wanting to do jobs only to please you and you both feeling the pressure to pursue jobs because of the investment of time and money. In most cases, a parent is much better suited for working alongside a manager or agent and simply being Mum or Dad looking out for their best interests and seeing the bigger picture as opposed to being deeply rooted in the business of industry and getting jobs.

I once offered to represent a child on an International job in Spain for a parent whose child was spotted on the street for a job. She said no, mainly because she wanted to keep all of the money and not pay me my 20%. The child ended up getting injured on set and being sent home, and she didn't know how to deal with the situation. If she had an agent to fight her corner, they would have got to the bottom of exactly what happened and established the best course of treatment for the child, instead of being kicked off the job and sent home.

Remember, production teams are on a budget, and more often than not if you are representing your own child, you are open to being paid less if you are not very clear on what should be paid and how to get the deal you want. I have also experienced it the other way where parents are too finically demanding and make expensive diva-ish requests and demand unreasonable fees. This is a massive turn off! The industry is small, and you usually find that kids with such parents do not get much work. Naming no names but I know there are a ton of parents out there who are seen as 'a nightmare' in the industry. You see, it's important to look out for your child, but don't be annoying! Remember good agents support parents too! It is not just about the kids.

Excuse Me...

I'm sure at some stage you have been out shopping or somewhere and been told how beautiful your child is. Perhaps, you may have even been approached by an agent to sign with them. I approach people when out all the time! Sometimes, casting directors approach parents directly too! If you have an agent and someone approaches you, your first port of call should always be them. They will assess the opportunity and handle everything for you. Trying to cut the agent out and handling it yourself is not cool for several reasons. One, you won't have the support if your child does get the job and will have to handle the whole process yourself. Two, there are a lot of scammers out there, and you do not want to be a victim of their next 'project'. Three, it's not good for the relationship with your agent if you go behind their back and cut them out for the sake of a commission. Yes, you may have to give them a cut of earnings, but the chances are they will make you more money on this job and future jobs if you are open with them.

TV Talent Shows

This topic is probably a book in itself! I am sure you have watched the numerous big TV talent shows that grace our screens year after year. There is no denying that their popularity has created massive International brands. Every year, kids grace our screens showcasing their talents, and the most successful ones end up launching very lucrative careers. Take UK dance troop Diversity, for example, the relatively unknown dance troop from Essex who didn't even win Britain's Got Talent, but went on to achieve success beyond their wildest dreams, selling out stadium tours and earning millions in endorsement deals, partnerships, merchandise, appearances, spin-off TV shows, and more. Some may be quick to point out that the Mum of the main dancer managed the group! She did indeed, but she is an ex-dancer, dance school owner, and represented other children at the time of the win! Perfect for them!

TV talent shows can be a great way for your child to be 'discovered.' However, it is important not to forget that they are a TV show and their main purpose is to entertain. Rejection is hard to bare anyway, but experiencing it in public can be even harder. So before entering, you will need to consider the effect it will have on your child and if they (and you) are ready for it. Be warned that the celebrity judges that you see on these shows do not see everyone. If you enter, you will have to audition to a production team first before moving forward to the celeb judging panel. It is a long process, and you will have to be very committed if you make it through to even the celeb judging rounds. Sometimes there are up to three auditions before that. If you get on to the show, there is also press attention to consider.

If you have an agent already, discuss with them before applying and they should help you manage the process if they feel it's appropriate. You never know, they may even be able to open doors for you. If you don't have an agent and are going it alone, just be sure to go into it with your eyes wide open. Know that it will take time and money initially to travel to necessary auditions and perhaps rehearsals and be prepared to put in lots of time and effort. Once on the show, you will have an obligation to that show so be sure to ask questions, read contracts, and get second opinions.

Make Me Instagram Famous Mama!

It is no secret that we now live in a digital age, and as a result of social media, your child can become 'famous' pretty much overnight. I'm sure you've seen those accounts of babies and even dogs with thousands of Twitter and Instagram. Having an account for your little one is now more popular than ever before. Now, before you begin posting perfect pics of your little protégé, there is much to consider. The moment you put your child out into the public domain on social media, they are open to the same criticism that any of us are open to when we share our lives openly. Is this something both you and your child can cope with? Especially in the beginning, public critiquing can be very tough to deal with. In my opinion, having your child on Instagram or a social media network should only be done with a strategic purpose in mind and if your child (NOT YOU) loves and enjoys what they are doing. Perhaps you want to showcase their modelling career, or they might have a particular skill you want to showcase.

Social media is amazing for getting recognised by the door openers and opportunity makers in most industries and gaining contacts and building relationships that can help to catapult your child's career. Accounts should always be managed by an adult, a parent, or agent if appropriate, and a child should never be allowed to engage with people online through a social media account simply because it's unsafe. If your child's account becomes popular enough you may start to receive offers for them to act as a brand ambassador. There is almost always a financial element to such deals, and they need to be handled by an adult.

As your child grows up and becomes more tech-savvy or is a teenager, they may have already created or want to create a social media account or YouTube channel. This can make it harder to manage, but it's vital that you still do. There are lots of kids that have gone on to achieve international fame and generate seven-figure incomes before adulthood by becoming a YouTube sensation. Truth is, a 'YouTuber' is a valid career now, and perhaps your child dreams of following in the footsteps of the likes of Tiana (Toys and me) who has six million subscribers and Chase's Corner who has on average 25 million views per video. They do not manage their own accounts and have someone, sometimes teams in place, to manage content and deal with queries and bookings. Social media management is a full-time job. It is important that kids remain kids and are protected at all times.

A client created his own YouTube channel which has received well over 1 million views. His Mum was astounded when he began to get calls to endorse products, companies, etc… and at this point, at age 14, he was managing the account entirely by himself.

Here are some top tips for managing your child's social media.

1. Ensure that you are in full control of the account. Decide if your child is mature enough to know the passwords.
2. Check the direct messages and emails every day for any opportunities. Never have your child do it. When getting in touch never agree to pay money. If it's an endorsement opportunity research the brand before giving over your address for sending merchandise or products.
3. Beware of scammers, people posing as talent agents who try to sell you a very expensive photo shoot.
4. Ensure your child understands that social media likes and comments are not a reflection of their talent or their ability. It does not mean that others are more beautiful than you just because they have more 'likes' and 'comments.'
5. Take all comments with a 'pinch of salt' … There are some mean people online who say silly things. Know what is worth sharing with your child and what is not.

> *"Knowledge is power and you need power in this world. You need as many advantages as you can get!" - Ellen Degeneres*

CHAPTER 3

NOT TOO COOL FOR SCHOOL

The fact that you have a future star on your hands is zero excuse for their commitment (and yours) towards their education to slip. Now I fully understand that not every child is academic, and that is fine, but they are still obliged to pursue academic studies, and their career will benefit from them being a well-educated individual in the long run.

Most children attend 'regular school' whether private or state and attend dance or theatre school in the evenings or on weekends. This is a totally valid route into the industry and attending full-time stage school is not a prerequisite to a successful career, however, for those with the financial means and children who have a distinct passion for the arts full-time, theatre or stage school might be an option for you.

Some full-time vocational schools accept children from as young as ten and tend to follow a timetable similar to that of the world-renowned Sylvia Young Theatre School in London and Dubai. Students follow an academic curriculum three days a week which includes academic subjects such as English, math, and science. For the other two days, they follow a vocational curriculum where they focus on performance skills including singing, dancing of all different styles, and drama. Audition technique is often covered in drama classes in stage school but would not be covered in a regular school. A stage school will, of course, be more relaxed about attending auditions and working during school time and will often grant time off for this with ease given the nature of the school.

Attending stage school usually comes with a fee. Typically, within the region of £5000 a term. Your child will need to audition to get accepted into the school too. School lunches are sometimes charged separately and can be in the range of £250 per term. Most stage schools have an agency attached to their school which means that they can manage your child's work diary and inform you of auditions when they arise too. Most stage schools offer a scholarship program where they give a place away to the most talented each year. Scholarship programs are usually hugely oversubscribed, require references and a lengthy audition process but if awarded a scholarship the benefits can be amazing. If you get a fee scholarship be aware that this is just for tuition, you will still have to purchase uniforms, pay for travel, lunches, and school supplies, so it is important you establish what's involved before accepting a scholarship.

There are some performing arts schools who do not charge fees because they are funded or set up as charities. Competition to get into these is fierce, but if your child is super passionate and more vocational education is what they truly desire, it is certainly worth trying.

Stage school does what it says on the tin. While academic studies are important, you must remember that for a whole two days vocational training is all that is on the curriculum and ultimately stage training is at the heart of what is offered. There will be greater investments of time and of course, money for fees, uniform, educational trips, and dance shoes. So, it is vital you get all the costs before signing up. You also need to be sure that your child really wants to pursue the arts before signing up to stage school, not just for financial reasons but to ensure they are happy at school and studying subjects that reflect their future career ambitions. For this reason, I am inclined to believe that stage school is better suited to older students, say 14 and older, once they have had a chance to evaluate what they truly want. However, it is very much a personal choice, and some children attend stage school from primary school, some even from nursery and go on to do very well academically and in their vocational career.

The great thing about stage school is the understanding that is had when time off is needed for auditions. In fact, most stage schools have their own agencies which students are often required to be a part of. Many stage schools offer on-site audition preparation sessions prior to auditions and castings which are super helpful. There is also more leniency with authorised absences for castings and due to the nature of their studies and the ethos of the school which prioritises performing and supports their student's early careers in the industry. Stage school should not be embarked on because a child wants to bypass academic study. It must be understood that any school is required to carry out the legal hours of education needed by a child by law. This may vary from country to country and state to state.

When choosing a stage school, it is important to look at the standard of academic education as well and ensure that your child will be fully supported in both areas. Although there is a heavy focus on their vocational studies they will still benefit from gaining basic level education if nothing else, as this will allow them to go on to further and higher education regardless of whether they 'make it' or not. Some kids are academic, and some are not, but a school that offers engaging lessons that will inspire your child to concentrate on math, English, and science as much as singing, dancing, and drama.

If full-time stage school is not for your child, but they still would like to have vocational training, then part-time theatre school or stage school is the way to go. There are schools that have a heavy focus on technique, some that are for fun and enjoyment, some for fitness, and some with a heavy performance or competitive focus. It is important that you find a school that suits the personality of your child. Historically, dance schools can be seen as quite 'cliquey' environments. Cue the 'Dance Moms' theme song, but you will find dance and stage schools around that have a real family vibe that doesn't compromise on training. It just might take some research and possibly some trial and error which is why most schools offer trial periods or classes which are free or cheaper than the cost of regular classes before you commit.

It's always good to get recommendations from friends and family who already attend performing arts establishments. Always remember what suits others may not suit you, but word of mouth is helpful when making such a personal decision. Some schools have classes on the weekend and some after school during the week. You may be required to attend on multiple days for different classes, so it is important to look at the entire commitment before making your choice. Financial investment is also important to consider. The cost of vocational training varies from free to thousands of pounds, so be sure to choose somewhere that is manageable, both in schedule and in cost. Also remember that there are likely to be other costs besides tuition that could include uniform, equipment, trips, exams, costumes, and shows.

Attending a part-time performing arts school is a great way for your child to build confidence and make friends who have similar interests. Sometimes, not everyone at school will understand their dreams and hopes for the future, but chances are friendships made at 'dance school' are friendships that will last for years to come. To this very day, I am friends with a couple of girls I grew up dancing with. It is also a great way for parents to network and build lasting friendships too. Not always but in some cases, more time is spent at the dance school than home on the weekends, so make sure you pick a place that has a feel of a second home and is welcoming and nurturing.

So, you've chosen a performance school, but now you have to choose the perfect class, and there are a ton to choose from. Knowing what style of class your child may like will help to make the decision about which school to choose a bit easier. My advice is to try all the classes during the trial period even if your child doesn't think they will like them as they may be pleasantly surprised.

Age classes will be for certain age groups regardless of ability. This has the benefit of your child being educated with children of a similar age range and emotional and intellectual maturity to themselves. However, be aware that ability can vary drastically. As long as the teacher has good skills in differentiating this within a class, mixed ability classes can work really well and create a community. On the other hand, classed grouped by ability are easier to run as everyone in the class is of a similar ability, and sometimes, classes are able to move at a faster pace for more advanced performers. Ability classes can be a little off-putting for children who are perhaps less able as they find themselves in a class with younger students which can sometimes discourage them from taking part.

In terms of styles of class, there will either be singing, drama, or dance based. Ballet is the foundation of all dance, so it is good if your child can take a ballet class, but no one style is essential. Any style they do should give them a sense of timing, musicality, and build confidence. Drama classes are not essential for working in entertainment, but they do sometimes give children a sense of presence that may help them in audition situations and on screen and stage.

Some directors prefer to work with children who have no prior acting training just bags of confidence as there is sometimes a chance that they will become 'over-trained', which then means they lose their raw and natural personality. It is their personality and how they bring that to a character that will get them a job over being 'false' and overacting. If musical theatre or singing is their thing, they will need to undergo some vocal training. Learning to use their voice safely and how to look after it is as important as learning to hit those high notes, so that is worth remembering too. Just like any school, it is important that you track their progress and take an interest in their development by regularly speaking to their teacher and supporting any work they need to do at home to practice routines, learn scripts or songs.

You will also need to decide if your child is most suited to group lessons or private lessons. Group lessons are great for building confidence and spatial awareness, they also have a social aspect to them. Private lessons are obviously less social, but they will get more attention and enable them to focus more on technique. Your school should advise you on the best route for you given the time you can commit to classes, your budget, and your child's long-term goals.

If you choose for your child to pursue a career in entertainment while they attend a 'regular school', you will need to have them fully on board for your child's career to work. You should talk to your child's teacher and the head teacher of the school before signing up to an agent to assess how supportive they will be. If your child is successful in obtaining a role, it is more than likely that they will require some time off from school. They will not be able to gain authorised absence without a written letter from the school. They may also need to catch up on work missed, which will mean the school will have to provide the work for them. Again, this will require the school to be very supportive of your child. Most schools usually are a great selling point for them if someone successful attends their school.

Having said that a school's main priorities are often attendance, punctuality, and academic results. If they feel that a career in entertainment would be detrimental to your child's studies no matter how young they are they are unlikely to support it. So to gain their support, it is important that your child has good attendance, usually over 95%, displays good behaviour, puts effort into their work, gets homework done on time and is punctual. It is also good for your agent to make contact with the school prior to any work undertaken. I have been to meetings with head teachers before to explain the industry in more detail and how having a job can affect a child's education. If they are aware of the demands and what's required they are in a much better position to support your child and you throughout the process.

FIVE TIPS TO ENSURE ACADEMIC STUDIES DO NOT SLIP

1. Still value education. It's important that they see you placing value on going to school and continuing with their academic studies regardless of how successful they are on stage or screen.
2. Keep open communication with their class teacher, so you are fully aware of their progress.
3. Encourage your child to look at books, have a look at magazines or even comics that interest them.
4. Encourage your child to tell you if there are things they are struggling with at school
5. Access support if necessary. Saturday school or extra tuition.

If your child gets a job which will require them to have time off school, they will need to make up the required weekly teaching with a personal tutor on the set of the project they are working on. Most of the time, the tutor is provided by production and is a qualified teacher with experience teaching working children. Your child will not learn in a conventional way. If there are other children on set, teaching may be carried out in small groups or pairs. If they are the only child, it will be one-to-one teaching. Lessons will take place around the shoot, so you can expect your child to film something and do some schoolwork during downtime of half an hour or more. There is no set time for this to happen as long as the required amount of hours (which varies from country to country) is carried out over the period of time, the child is working. This sometimes means making up the hours after the shoot has finished. Each minute your child spends with the tutor is calculated and recorded on their time sheet to ensure they get the required hours in.

Prior to the shoot commencing make contact with the tutor and arrange for them to contact your child's school. Tutoring on set works best when there is a partnership between that tutor and your child's teachers. It's awesome if the school can provide work to ensure that your child is following the curriculum, will not be behind when they return to school and working on things that are relevant. It is also a good idea to have a reading book to accompany any work too so that they keep their reading up and books are a great time filler between scenes if working in television. Always take more work from the school as you will sometimes be surprised at how quickly kids get through the work. Better to have too much than too little. Sometimes schools are not keen to give out work for various reasons.

In this case, the tutor should provide age-appropriate work for your child. You should be sure to see this work to make sure it is suitable and actually going to stretch and benefit your child, and they will learn. Sometimes tutor time will be used for educational visits, especially if your child is on tour. Now, trips to the local museum are cool and can be good for your child to learn about their surroundings. Especially since while working, the only thing they will get to see is a dance studio, a couple of restaurants, and the theatre. Having said this trips should not be used as an easy option for tutor time which means no actual writing and school work gets done. The trips need to be in moderation and relevant not five trips per week to the park during tutor time. Trips to the park should be during recreation time.

If your child is on a long-term job be sure to have a good relationship with the tutor and ensure they provide feedback to the school on what work has been done, return completed work and ask for more before the current work runs out. Tutoring works best when the conversation is three ways between the school, tutor, and parent. Production should also be aware of any challenges, special educational needs or upcoming examinations to allow your child to have a tutor who is best suited to them and support them accordingly. I have experienced a 12-year-old child doing a colouring book during tutor time for a week simply because no one had checked so I cannot stress enough the importance of forming a strong partnership with the school, tutor, and production as well as speaking to your child.

As with much of the entertainment industry your child will probably naturally take on more responsibility for themselves; this includes their education. Performing kids get so familiar with what's required of them you often find them calculating the hours themselves and not having to be told to do their schoolwork. This is great as they are keen to complete their schoolwork. Their tutor time is a break away from the set on longer jobs. However, some kids hate academic studies and will do anything to get out of them. They love being on set but not so keen on the classroom. It's important that your child knows the value of education and how it fits in with their vocational career. Have a conversation with your child about the importance of being knowledgeable and how it will aid them in acting roles. The more they know, the better informed they will be to play a wider variety of roles. Math is important for working out finances and literacy for understanding contracts. If they struggle with academia, try to relate everything back to what they love.

I have known parents in the past to get a tutor who works with their child on weekends when they are not on set to ensure that their studies do not suffer. This is fine for some, but it is not for everyone. You will be able to gauge based on work completed and conversations with your child's tutor how they are getting on if they are out of school for prolonged periods. It is also important to remember that they will have to return to school eventually and school is not all academics. Where possible make sure they maintain their friendships and speak to their school friends, so they are still part of the school community. Some schools even arrange trips to screenings and theatre shows if a child is on a long-term project. Just check beforehand to ensure it's what your child wants to avoid any added pressure for them to perform if they are working on a live show.

Wicked Workshops!

It is still important that your child keeps their training up while working. Yes, they will be learning all sorts of skills on the job, but it is important they keep up with training when their schedule permits. Skill-specific workshops are a great way to do this. Whether they are on a job or not, it is useful to attend workshops. Especially those hosted by your agent as they are often attended by casting directors, and you'll be able to get great feedback for your child on what they need to work on as well as learning short scripts and working with others. The So You Think Your Kid's Got Talent workshops have separate workshops for parents with a question and answer session. It is important that you as a parent know how to support your child best through this process, parent workshops can provide clarity plus you get to mix with other parents who have children who have similar interests and to ask questions and learn from them.

FIVE TIPS TO HELP YOU CHOOSE THE PERFECT STAGE SCHOOL -from a Stage School Mum

1. Decide what is important to you in terms of shows, competitions, technique and choose a school with a heavy focus on this.
2. Be sure you can afford it before you start; the uniform, the trips, the costumes, and shows. Get an estimated cost for all items and ensure it fits your budget.
3. Do not join a stage school just because a friend or family member goes there. Kids fall out, and they may not end up in the same class anyway. So attend because they truly want to.
4. Try to have a chat with the teachers that will be teaching your child; it's good to get a feel of their expectations and how they structure classes.
5. It's always nice to get feedback and views of others who may have attended the school but go with your gut, once you have visited the school and you and your child are happy with the classes that's the main thing.

"The only failure is not to try."
- George Clooney

CHAPTER 4

AWESOME AUDITIONING

Before your child even gets to an audition, they need to make sure they are mentally and physically prepared. This means making sure that your child gets a good night sleep before the audition. Make sure they eat a healthy meal and are well hydrated. You don't want them to feel sluggish and tired for their audition.

In addition to being physically and emotionally prepared, there will typically be a certain amount of material preparation that is required. Your child may be given something to learn beforehand, a script, a song or you may have to perform a certain skill I have heard of everything from stacking cups to riding a bike. If this is the case, your agent will inform you of this and provide any scripts or info you need. Sometimes it is necessary for you to prep your own material. Speak to your agent or performing arts tutor for guidance. There are lots of monologues available online for every age group just type 'monologues for (insert age) group' into a search engine, and you'll find loads, or your child can often recite their favourite poem or piece of prose. If you are not given anything, then your child will be told what to do on the day. It is worth them learning a song really well and a poem or monologue so that when auditions come up, there is something they know really well. Don't make this overly complicated. A nursery rhyme or happy birthday are completely acceptable songs.

On a practical note before you accept the audition make sure you can make the audition in terms of timing. You will be told the production dates so make sure you can also commit to all of those dates as well. If you have a holiday booked, you will need to be willing to cancel it with no compensation if your child is successful at gaining the role. If you cannot commit to the dates, speak to your agent who will advise, but it will probably be the case that your child will not go to the audition to avoid a clash in dates of prior engagements. You will also receive information about what the job entails in terms of storyline.

It is important that you are comfortable with the storyline also in terms of content. Could be hard-hitting storylines that deal with adult issues like drugs. Some parents also do not want their children associated with certain brands. It is important to remember that it is acting, but you have the right to have your beliefs and not have your child exposed to certain issues through their work. However, you should let your agent know from the outset what you are comfortable with and they will not put your child forward for certain roles that involve certain storylines. Especially with older children and teens, it is important they feel comfortable taking on certain roles and are reassured about how a particular storyline will be handled.

The million-dollar question…what should they wear? Unless your child has been told to wear something specific, they should wear something comfortable that they can easily move in. If it's a dance audition, you will definitely want to pack their sneakers or dance shoes. If you are coming straight from school casting directors are usually ok with school uniforms. Hair should be neat and tidy, and their face should look as natural as possible. No makeup on younger ones and if teenagers must wear makeup keep it a very natural look with a clear lip balm. The casting director wants to see a natural child. Makeup often makes kids look older, and that's not appropriate.

Once you have tackled what to wear, you need to make sure you have everything you need for the audition. If you are unsure of what else to bring, ask your agent. They can let you know if you need to bring a headshot, portfolio, resume, script, prop, or anything else. There is no need to bring any of it if your agent doesn't tell you to. They usually have all this information emailed to them beforehand. They can also let you know what to expect in terms of length of time for the audition, the number of kids auditioning, and when to expect a response.

Different types of casting are going to require different preparation. For modelling castings, establish if it's a photographic also known as stills job or catwalk. For catwalk jobs, your child should practice freestyle dancing and walking with confidence and purpose with their head lifted, shoulders back, a straight back and often plenty of sass! For stills, the ability to be relaxed and take direction is what is important, so it's harder to prep for. Taking a million selfies will probably not help your child. You should make sure that your child is very familiar with the job. What is it for? Is there any information they need to know? This could be the theme of the shoot. For example, is it for Halloween? If it's a continuing drama, what are the current themes and headlines and how does the character they are auditioning for fit in? And also, it's worth (especially for older children) researching, the director or any actors already cast for context and so they can engage in conversation confidently about the project, plot, or characters. Audition prep is supposed to be fun! Don't put too much pressure on it, but still make sure that your child has the required knowledge to approach the audition.

One important thing to understand is that every audition is different. Depending on the job and the way the casting director arranges their casings. It's not a one size fits all. An audition is a casting director's opportunity to meet and get to know you a little in order to assess if you will fit the requirements for a certain role. Auditions vary in length, and they are sometimes conducted in small groups and sometimes individually. You never get a ton of notice about auditions. They are historically last minute.

Your child may be given something to learn beforehand, a script, a song, or you may have to perform a certain skill. I have heard of everything from stacking cups to riding a bike. If you are not given anything, then your child will be told what to do on the day. When you get to an audition, there will usually be a bit of paperwork to complete before your child heads in. It will ask for pretty basic info and contact details as well as details of your agent if you have one. Parents are seldom ever allowed in the audition room with the exception of babies. There are usually licensed chaperones on hand to accompany your child into the audition room and whilst they are in there. Space is often pretty tight, so it's always a good idea to only take a child that is auditioning. There isn't always much space for prams or additional relatives.

Do not be alarmed if your child is out of the audition as quick as they are in. This does not mean that they have not got the part, especially if there are quite a few children there. The team will usually have taken enough footage and photos to establish if they would like to pursue things with your child and for quick auditions, you will often find there will be another opportunity to meet before any decisions are made. My advice is to take a book to read or something else to do, just in case you are there for a while.

At auditions, you are as much on audition as your child. Casting directors don't want to work with parents who they anticipate will make their life harder or cause them any kind of headache. Please understand that this does not mean you don't ask questions if you do not understand something immediate but be mindful of audition etiquette. If you have an agent, it is best to address your questions to them after the audition or if it's something important, call them (discretely) or text them while you are there, and they will ask questions on your behalf, or they may even have the answers.

Remember that at auditions, you do not know who is who. Do not discuss your dissatisfaction about something to others around you even if you think they are 'just other Mums' again, speak to your agent. There is sometimes a 'my child is better than your child' culture in audition waiting rooms. Whilst I would always advise you to be polite, you do not feel you have to disclose information about your child to the other parents and engage in a 'boasting match' if that's not something you want. Likewise, you do not know who is who, so if you are dissatisfied with something save it for your agent or a private email. 'Public mouthing off' is not a good look either! There may be long waits, standing around, and crowded waiting areas but complaining to whoever will listen could cost your child the job if it is perceived as 'bitching or moaning.'

You may find that your child is asked to do a 'self-tape' audition. Self-tape means that your child will be asked to do a task at home and you will film them doing that task. That video will then be submitted to the casting director for consideration. Self-tape audition tasks can include things like a scene from the production they are auditioning for, simply introducing themselves to the camera, or saying what they like to eat. They may be asked to do a skill like play football or ride a bike. Be sure to do self-tapes against a plain background if it's just a speaking audition. If there is a script involved, say the lines that don't apply to your child off camera. The casting director will not want to see you unless it's relevant to the job.

With self-tapes, you are in control. Videoing on your phone is fine, and you can do it a few times and then choose the best one to send. I recommend doing it three times, as too many times and mistakes start to happen. Make sure you think about your surroundings when you film and make sure all other noise is to a minimum. Don't have younger siblings talking or crying in the background and be sure to tell your child to speak up. Self-tape auditions are a good introduction to auditioning as they allow kids to audition in the comfort of their own environment. However, engagements or roles are rarely cast straight from self-tape auditions. There will typically be a second and sometimes even a third audition before your child is cast in the part. It is important that with self-tapes you follow all the instructions given and please don't let your child record the audition in their pyjamas! It's not a good look! Treat the self-tape like you would in a live audition. You don't have to stress out about it, just approach it with the same professionalism you would have in any other audition.

However your child auditions for a role, your role as a parent should be one of complete support. Auditioning for anything takes grit and guts! I remember feeling super nervous going to auditions as a child. Luckily, I had the type of Mum who would say just try your best and that's good enough. There was never any pressure to get the job. It very much felt like I wanted the opportunity more than her, which is how I think it should be. Remember, if you are flustered your child will be too! That nervous energy rubs off! Make sure you never put pressure on the outcome of the audition. The most important thing is that your child is relaxed, has fun, and enjoys the experience. Make sure they know that as much as they want the opportunity, whatever happens, is fine. You need to be a source of encouragement with a can-do attitude. Empower them to be the best they can be and while remaining positive let them know the reality of the opportunity they are going for.

I find a good way is after the audition to tell them that they have done amazingly well to get an audition and that the outcome of any audition is not purely based on talent it sometimes has to do with a lot of other factors that are beyond their control. For example, it may depend on who has already been cast. From my experience, the kids who are most successful at auditions have parents who are super laid back about the outcome and support their child through the entire process while keeping their feet firmly on the ground by giving them the 'supportive reality check.' Remember this is their dream, and they want this for themselves. You just need to support them.

Chances are that sooner or later you will experience a callback. A 'callback' is another word for a second audition. There are not always callbacks, but quite often casting teams will whittle down their options from a long list and ask to see your child again if they are interested in casting them. You might find they are invited back to two or three 'callbacks' before a final decision is made. Obviously, it is fantastic if they do get a callback, but it is important to remember that they are still firmly in the audition stage so that they try just as hard at the callback as they did the first time around.

On a callback more often than not they will be asked to do something they will have to do if they are successful at gaining the role. This could be meeting an on-screen family they would be part of, reading an actual script from a show, or eating a bowl of cereal if it is an advert for frosted flakes. Be sure to support them with the prep and mentally, as well as, emotionally prepare them. Explain the callback process. The way you tell them needs to be age appropriate, but essentially, they need to understand that they are through to the next round which is a positive thing, but they have not gotten the job just yet.

Sometimes you may be able to get direction and feedback on something they can do differently or work on for the callback auditions. If there is material for them to learn, support them with this in the same way. At a callback phase, you may want to consult a performance coach to work on a specific element of their performance. This is usually most useful if they have a song to learn. Kids can grow in confidence in just one session! If they have a regular singing teacher, I would suggest maybe a one-to-one session with them. Again, remember to remain positive throughout the entire callback phase and approach it the same as you did the first audition.

After the callbacks, casting decisions start to be made, and kids are 'penciled' for jobs. Now, it's really important that this terminology is understood. Penciled does NOT mean a child has the job. Pencil can be easily erased. It means that the team is very interested in casting your child, but there are other factors that still need to be worked out. This could also include casting others that will work alongside your child, deciding if they have enough budget to cast your child, working out if the schedule can accommodate a child on set. They also like to have options, so perhaps they haven't finished casting yet but really like your child.

This phase is also referred to in the industry as 'optioning.' It is really important that you do not get your hopes up and think that your child has the job until it has been confirmed. It is of course entirely your decision if you tell your child they are penciled. I know lots of parents do not tell their kids until a decision has been confirmed. If you do tell them I would word it as they have 'reached the final stages'.

The worst thing you can do is tell them they have the job because you may find yourself in a situation where you have to take that back, and it does happen! In fact, it happens a lot! People change their mind, things happen, and sometimes projects fall through. So, it's important that hopes are not raised unnecessarily. Being penciled or optioned is still a fab achievement, and the positives of that should be focused on if you tell your child. But I repeat, please do not go around saying they have the job until it has been officially confirmed!

CASTING DIRECTORS TOP 5 TIPS FOR AUDITIONING

1. Keep calm and take a deep breath before you start.
2. Bring a bottle of water.
3. Be sure to be prepared, read over any text sent before coming.
4. Know what job or part you are going for.
5. Have fun. If you enjoy yourself, you will do a better performance

A PERFORMING CHILD'S TOP 5 TIPS FOR AUDITIONING

1. Be yourself!
2. Make sure you practice any lines or songs
3. Make sure you remind your parent to bring anything you may need with you.
4. Speak up and don't be shy.
5. Don't worry if you don't get the job, just keep trying.

"Be so good they can't ignore you."
-Steve Martin

CHAPTER 5

THEY'VE GOT THE JOB!

Remember that pencil their name was written in? Well, it's now in pen, and they have officially got the job! Eeek! This is obviously all kinds of exciting, and now the hard work and fun truly begin. You will usually find out your child has got a job via your agent. This is standard protocol.

I have known of few productions who contact parents directly. However, as exciting as it all is, always ask production to liaise with your agent as it's their job to negotiate deals and make sure that your child gets the most out of being involved in the production. They will also be responsible for the paperwork, so it's important that they are involved from day one. It is also much better for your child, for production to know you value your agent and that they must deal with them as it keeps things professional and sets a precedence for communication for the duration of the job.

This is still not the time to jump on social media and make big announcements. A lot of projects are press-embargoed, which means no one can talk about them until a certain date. So as excited as you are, be sure to check before you let the cat out of the bag! That would be very embarrassing for all and is a simple mistake to avoid. In extreme cases it could result on your child losing out on the job before they have even started, you can also damage relationships with producers, which could prevent future opportunities, so it is really not a good idea.

Once you have found out your child has the job and you have accepted it, your agent will begin to negotiate a contract on behalf of your child. This contract will determine things like payment for them, chaperone fees for you, schedule, and expectations. You will also have an idea of the filming dates, your child's wages, and commitment needed for the project before auditioning, but a good agent will always try to negotiate the best deal for your child in terms of fees and length of time on set.

It will not always be possible to get more money, but sometimes they can get what I call 'comfort add-ons' which are things like cars to pick you up and drop you off to set or reimbursement for travel. If there is something you would like in particular, then let your agent know. Bear in mind that you need to keep requests reasonable. No requests for luxury restaurant catering, or only blue M&Ms, or scented designer candles. You probably won't get them, and you and your child will be seen as difficult divas, no one wants to work with people like that so you can kiss goodbye to being recast.

This is probably also a good time to mention that you can't miss a day of filming or ask for things to be moved around because a kid's party has come up. Once a contract is agreed to, it is important that you stick to the dates. A shoot or production has a lot of people involved which often has a high cost associated with it, dates have to be stuck to. You and your agent will not be looked on kindly if you pull out of a date once agreed which may make it difficult to get more work going forward. Things like serious illness cannot be helped, but generally, once the contract has been negotiated and signed, the work needs to be carried out and on schedule.

Depending on where in the world you live the work permit or child licensing application procedure will be slightly different. However, the purpose of obtaining a work permit or license for your child is the same wherever you live. The purpose of the permit is for the government to be assured that production companies are doing the right thing by the kids they have working on their projects. Licenses need to be applied for and be processed before any child under 16 carries out any paid or sometimes unpaid work.

During the application process, the production will be checked for health and safety on set, and their arrangement for adequate supervision of all of the working children involved will be reviewed. There will be an assessment of their risk management plan, their tutoring arrangements, and the schedule of the children's working hours will be assessed to ensure that they are meeting government requirements. For exacts hours and requirements, contact your local borough council who will give you information on the Child Employment Act which is what the entertainment rules are based on.

It is important that you are clear on the hours of work that are legally acceptable and the breaks your child will need to have in between. If laws that relate to child employment are broken, the whole production could be in jeopardy, and the project can be shut down. For some productions, that could be the cost of millions of dollars wasted because rules have not been followed. The child employment laws are put in place to protect your child while they are working. If they are over-working it may cause them to over-tired, which means they get ill or under perform. If you suspect child employment laws are not being followed and you are on set in the capacity of a chaperone you should speak to your designated contact. If not, then speak to your agent who will raise this with production on your behalf.

The script will also be checked for the suitability of the storyline involving children and the schedule of the shoot will be checked to ensure that it doesn't interfere with a child's education, which is usually through the provision of a tutor if away from school for long periods. It is during this stage that sometimes details of the script that may not have been previously disclosed come to light. For example, nighttime shoots or maybe something like a stunt they want your child to perform such as horse riding or skateboarding. The possibilities are endless. If there are stunts to perform, do not worry. In my experience, lessons are provided before filming and if anything was ever deemed unsafe or your child seemed uneasy they would use a stunt double. Encourage your child to be open and honest about how they feel about the emoluments of scripts and stunts.

One time a client of mine found out that they would need to pick their nose for a commercial, she was filming while her work license was being processed. This was flagged for the council and swiftly removed from the script. Can you imagine the impact that it would have on the child at school, to be seen on National TV time and time again picking their nose? Yes, they want the limelight, but it is important to think of the impact of playing certain roles will have on their everyday life. Especially, with today's technology where once something is out there, it cannot be erased.

A question I get asked regularly is about what children see if the show they are in is for adults. There may be scenes relating to violence, sex, or drugs. TV and film are not filmed in sequence, and in my experience, children never see those scenes. It is at the discretion of your local council to decide if the overall topic of the show is suitable for children to be in. They will also take into account the dialogue which may contain swearing or illicit content. There will be conditions in place to protect your child while filming, just bare in mind when it airs the overall topic of the show will be expressed and that they would not have seen that during the filming. It has happened before where certain scenes come to light only when the show has been aired, and neither the young actors nor the chaperones had any idea that those concepts were even in the show.

Instead of writing out each country's rules (because it would be a book in itself and probably a tad boring to read through), contact your local borough council office who will inform you of the exact requirements for your area.

Rules on child employment in the USA vary from state to state. Check out the requirements for each state here: https://www.dol.gov/whd/state/childentertain.htm

For Australia, check out this link: http://www.business.vic.gov.au/hiring-and-managing-staff/employing-children/laws-and-act

For the UK, check out this booklet from the department of education that takes you through the child employment laws: /www.gov.uk/government/uploads/system/uploads/attachment_data/file/387940/Child_Performance_Regulations_report_of_the_consultation_on_performance_hours_and_breaks.pdf

The thing to always remember about licenses is that it is a legal requirement for your child to work. If the license doesn't come through in time, then your child can not legally work on that project. However, don't fret. Your agent will help to navigate the application process. It is worth noting your local council office's lead times to ensure that you will get the license in time for your child to do the job. I have seen on more than one occasion where children miss out on opportunities because the council couldn't complete the license in time.

Once the licensing and permits are all squared, it is important to establish whether you will be allowed on set or backstage. Some productions and jobs will prefer you to chaperone your own child and others will not. If you are asked to chaperone your own child, you need to take into account what the production is willing to pay you, and you will have to take some time off work. Remember that being a chaperone is a professional job. The chaperones responsible for caring for your children on any project will have undergone safeguarding training and should have a good knowledge of the child employment laws. This is to ensure that the law is being followed whilst your child is working. It is a good idea that you become a licensed chaperone, so you can learn the law too. To do this, you will need to contact your local council or borough office.

On set, a chaperone's duty is to ensure the well-being of your child. A chaperone's loyalty is to your child to ensure they are safe, they get their required breaks, and they ask questions about actions your child may have to carry out. Good chaperones say no to directors if a child safety will be compromised or they have gone over the amount of hours they are legally allowed to film or perform in a day. They keep records of what your child does on a daily basis and has to present these reports to the authorities should they do a spot check.

If your child is going on tour, you should meet the chaperone prior to the start date. This is your opportunity to get to know them a bit. On tour, there will be more than one chaperone although one person is usually assigned to your child. Phones are not allowed on set, so get the phone number of the chaperone so you can contact them if necessary. Production days are long and busy, so do not be alarmed if you do not hear from your child all day. Keep this in mind if contacting the chaperone too.

Most of the time there is a head chaperone who is 'in charge' of chaperoning duties. If you have a question or concern, generally this is the person you would contact. You should be given the number of chaperone assigned to your child and deal with them if there are any concerns. It is not a good idea to try to contact your child directly. Any conflicts between chaperone and child should be resolved as soon as possible. In my experience, this is rarely an issue but if a situation arises where there is an issue between your child and their chaperone speak to your agent who can set up a talk with the head chaperone and chaperone to resolve an issue. If a resolution cannot be found your child may be reassigned a chaperone at the discretion of production and dependent on the situation.

If the authorities come and do a spot-check of the production your child is working on, and they are not abiding by all the rules in relation to the safety of your child they can be shut down immediately. I have known of a massive production costing thousands of pounds to shoot that was shut down because there was not the correct ratio of chaperones to children. Another was shut down because a stunt they wanted a child to carry out was deemed unsafe.

Getting a job is an exciting time, but there is sometimes much to consider. Be sure to have a conversation with your child about the job they are taking on and explain how everything will work in terms of schooling, if they are filming away from home sit down and go through the schedule with them so that they feel reassured and comfortable. This might be a nice thing to do as a family, sharing the experience with everyone in the house so that siblings are aware of changes. Talk to them about changes they might see to their regular schedule. For example, they may have to accompany you after school to go and collect their sibling from the theatre. Approaching a job as a family helps to ease the pressure as everyone knows what is going on and siblings still feel part of the experience. Your agent should be able to help and support you with this talk if necessary.

"A career in showbiz is like a distance run, you have to have patience and pace yourself." - Unknown

CHAPTER 6

GREAT EXPECTATIONS

Now you probably have all these ideas of what it's like to work on a film set or in the theatre or on the catwalk. I am sure through watching various television shows your child also has their own ideas of what it's like. I hate to be the bearer of bad news but many a time working in showbiz although super fun is often not as glamorous as it looks. It is learning scripts, practicing routines, and working hard. Very hard. Quite often kids enjoy themselves so much that they don't see it as work at all!

It is important to remember that every child is different and will approach the world of showbiz in different ways. Some kids can't wait for their parents to leave when they drop them off on a set whereas others feel more reassured if you stick around. As mentioned in the previous chapter, some productions will not allow parents to chaperone their own children. You will need to respect this.

I find that kids behave differently and perform differently when their parents are around. So, as much as you want to be involved, in most cases, it's best you leave them to it on set as long as you are happy with the arrangements agreed on their license. If you do find yourself in a position where you are chaperoning your child, it is important to remember you are there to look after them and their interests. As tempting as it may be to capture every moment, your role is not to take photos of them at every given opportunity, record footage, or request photos with every celebrity in site! CRINGE!

None of the above will go down well with any production team. By all means, it is important to know the rules as you may be the only 'chaperone' on set and you need to make sure you are able to record your child's working hours and handle conversations with other members of the production team in a professional manner. You will be responsible for making sure your child is on set on time and following the schedule set out for them.

If you are on a job with your child, you will have to take a back seat but know if and when to step in for their own safety. Your child will need to take direction from the director who may speak in a manner that may sometimes not be 'sweet music' to your ears. It may be your natural reaction to defend your child, but you will have to stand back and let the director take the lead especially when filming TV shows. There is a lot of direction to take in. It's also not a great idea to fill them with a ton of direction and ideas because what you are telling them may conflict with what the production team has told them, and also, you need to be careful about overloading them and making them feel pressured.

On the rare occasion, you are allowed to be on set if there is a chaperone present, it is important that you let them do their job and just be there to observe. I have known parents to accompany their children on jobs every day and have to sit in a waiting lounge because they are not actually allowed on set. You will have to evaluate if this is feasible for you or not, as you will not see your child until the end of the day after shooting or rehearsals.

Sometimes, the cast will be predominantly kid based, and your child might be one of a large all child cast. This often happens with children's television shows or in the theatre. If your child is away from home, this will mean them having to make new friends with other cast members and sometimes, sharing a room with them. Just because it is an all child cast does not mean that expectations of behaviour are any less.

However, the normal issues which arise when a group of children comes together still come into play. These little squabbles are usually easily dealt with by the chaperones. Kids will be kids, and childish behaviour is to be expected. However, you have to remember that they are being paid to do a job. Time is money, and it will not be favoured to have to constantly stop and correct their behaviour or ask them to stop talking.

It is very important that as a parent you evaluate if you think your child displays the kind of behaviour which will enable them to cope in an environment where they will have to conform to rules which are sometimes different to home. This could be different bedtimes, mealtimes, or general expectations. The kids who do the best in this industry are able to adapt their behaviour in different situations and respond to instructions. It's important that they are able to do the right thing when others may not be behaving in an appropriate manner. There are no extra points for following the crowd. The industry is extremely small, and nobody wants to employ a child who won't behave.

I have known of a case where a child was actually fired from a job for not behaving. Ultimately, this was a case of a few incidences of unacceptable behaviour which built up during the weeks of rehearsal leading up to a National stage production that ended in a physical fight between him and another cast member. This was a lead character, it was the night before press night, and this child was asked to leave the show. Billboards were up, programs already printed, promotion had been done, and tickets had been bought, but after an altercation with another cast member, the production team made the decision to fire this young boy.

Now, you can imagine the upset that this caused the young actor, his family, and his agent. The company then had a logistical nightmare on their hands to replace the child and re-do everything his face appeared on. After I investigated the incident further, it turned out that the boy had been going through some issues at school and felt quite pressured. Not an excuse for his actions, but knowing that he was under stress and experiencing bullying at school explained why he had behaved in that way. Had his mother had known and raised this issue earlier, perhaps the team may have been able to manage the situation better which may have prevented the outcome.

Here is how you can help your child display the behaviour that will get them noticed for the right reasons on set.

1. If there have been any changes, at school or home, let someone on production know. Anything that may cause them to behave differently. If they are anxious or worried a lot of the time all it takes is a little reassurance for them to feel more comfortable.
2. Be sure to talk to your child about expectations for behaviour.
3. Ask production about any specific bedtimes, call times and mimic that at home before they go.
4. Be sure to inform production about dietary needs and likes and dislikes in a non-diva way, that way, they won't need to complain about the food. **Extra tip** - it is also helpful for production. If your child is gluten intolerant and has to eat a bowl of pasta as part of the job, special arrangements will need to be made.
5. Tell your child that juvenile behaviour of any type will not be welcome and acceptable!

The Harsh Reality

You may be reading this book because your little one dreams of seeing their name in the bright lights of Broadway or having a star on the Hollywood walk of fame! Whilst many parents will agree that the world of child entertainment is super fun and provides children with a world of opportunities they may not otherwise get; there are (as with everything) some downsides and things to consider before going ahead with a career in the entertainment industry.

When your child enters the world of showbiz, it's a life-changing experience without a doubt. They may miss school, be around adults a lot more often, and the industry really does mature them a lot quicker. This can sometimes make things difficult when socialising with peer groups at school. If they are away for long periods of time, they can sometimes feel 'left out' when they return and find it hard to integrate back into 'normal school life.' Not to mention that unfortunately some children can be very cruel and sometimes maybe even jealous, and it is not uncommon for kids in showbiz to face bullying. This may be at school or at their dance class.

You would hope that bullying would not happen at all, but if it were to occur your child needs to feel comfortable enough to report it to you. Luckily bullying is not something I have dealt with often. However, I have known parents to try to deal with the problem themselves. This is not the most effective way. Always inform your agent. Even if the bullying is happening at school. A good agent will help to resolve it which may mean speaking to the school, production team, and providing reassurance to your child too. I have had meetings with head teachers and set up mediation between children which has helped in the past. Remember, working is supposed to be a fun experience. Harassment or bullying is not part of the job. Remember to keep communicating with your child and be sure that they know that they need to let you or a chaperone know if someone is making them feel upset or uncomfortable.

In addition to the strains and stress being in show business adds on to the child, there is no doubt that having a working child will impact the rest of the family in some way. It is usually the case that your child might not have a job for a while and then the weekend of that family wedding- bam! A big opportunity. Navigating how your child will get to the job and to the wedding can be a very stressful experience. You need to be sure you have the support in place to accommodate the dropping off and picking up once they have the job. Will your work accommodate you leaving early, working through lunch, working from home to accommodate your child's career? Changes to schedules are a regular thing so notice that you need to leave early to pick up your child will often be short. The financial implications also need to be thought about because whilst you will more than likely be paid travel contributions, these often take a long time to process and you may have to fund travel for a while before they are reimbursed.

If you have other children, it will most definitely affect them too. If all your children are in the industry, it can be particularly hard if one child is getting more opportunities than the other. It is super important that all family members feel valued and part of the experience. While your working child is in rehearsals or on a shoot, that's an opportunity to grab a bite to eat or a hot chocolate and have some quality one-on-one time with your other children. Be sure there is open communication with all of your children and talk to them about their thoughts and feelings. Try to keep up with their activities. If you have the support that may mean one parent taking one of the kids to one activity and the other parent taking your other kid(s) to another. It can be tricky to juggle but very worthwhile.

I have known situations where siblings of children in the spotlight become very withdrawn, their schoolwork starts to suffer, and their behaviour changes almost as a way of rebelling and seeking attention. Be sure that your child's school knows the situation, so they can notify you of any changes if and when they arise so that you can deal with them and ensure that everyone is happy and supported.

An Account of a West End Mama…

When my Son first got cast in a West end, it was an incredibly exciting time for the whole family. He was getting the chance to live his dream of being on the big stage. He was in the show for eighteen months, as a single Mother this was tough with two other children to raise as well. At first, there really was a struggle. I felt like I lived life to ferry my son to and from the theatre. One of my other children became very resentful. It really hurt one day when she said that I loved my son more. That sparked a change in things. I began to tap into my network of family and friends who then started to help me with the dropping off and picking up. This allowed me to be home more for my other children, cook dinners, help with homework, and do housework. It began to really affect their behaviour at school, and they missed me. On days when I would take my son to the theatre, I made a rota once a fortnight that my daughters would come too and we would get dinner while he was at the theatre before picking him up. That gave us time to bond and still made them feel valued and important to me. Once I worked out a routine that worked for our family, we all started to really enjoy the process and were actually quite sad when it ended. Although the sadness was short-lived, as it meant we were able to go on holiday as a family! And then he got cast in another show.

Handling the Holidays

Holidays can be difficult to get too. If your child is in a continuous drama or lands a part in a musical as part of the contract, you will have to agree that you will not take any holidays during the time they are contracted with the company. Once agreed this has to be stuck to. Again it is worth considering the impact of not having family holidays will have on the rest of the family. One of my clients once booked a big family holiday to Florida and got cast in a serial drama. They forfeited the holiday, lost that money for their child to do the show. There are families who go on holiday without the performing child. Letting them stay with someone else while they go. There is no right or wrong way, it's about considering all of these things and working out what is best for you and your family. Communication is key.

"Perseverance is failing 19 times and succeeding the 20th"
- Julie Andrews

CHAPTER 7

WHEN THEIR GORGEOUS FACES JUST DON'T FIT

It's no secret that your child will not get every job they are put up for. It's vital that both you and your son or daughter are ok with that. It can sometimes be disappointing, but every cloud has a silver lining. If it can be established why they did not get the job, which it sometimes can, it can really help them improve their performance and maybe even help them to get a similar job next time. The hardest part is there may not be a distinct reason, and quite often the reason may be that their face just doesn't fit. In an age of Instagram selfies and Snapchat, it is super important that rejection of this kind is managed in the right way. Your child should never feel pressure to lose weight, put on weight, or that the colour or texture of their hair or the colour of their skin is disadvantageous. I often say to my own young clients that the part is not right for them, never that they are not right for a part. Kids need to be encouraged to feel comfortable in their own skin. This confidence will allow them to do better auditions and develop unwavering self-belief which is so important in the competitive world of show business.

The Magic of Rejection

Rejection is an ineffable part of the audition process. The harsh reality is that most kids will not get a job! (Not trying to put you off.) There are hundreds and sometimes, thousands going for the same job. At this stage, you may think "well what's the point then?" But the truth is someone does get the job and that someone may be your child. I've seen children go to audition after audition and travel far and wide to castings and getting constant rejections. The ones who are the most successful have often attended a ton of auditions before getting their big break. It is unrealistic to expect to go for your first audition, get it and become an international superstar. (It does happen) but it's more likely to be a longer process before your child gets their first job.

One of the first clients I ever took on auditioned for twenty-two things before they secured a role in a TV show. It was fantastic that they kept going. I give their parents so much credit for this child's eventual success as they still managed to instill a 'can do' attitude in their child even through continuous disappointment.You see, rejection can become draining for you as a parent as much as the child, perhaps even more. With more life experience comes more feelings, but it is important that your own feelings around rejection do not rub off on your child. It is also tiring ferrying your kids up and down the City and sometimes even the country if it seems like you are not getting anywhere.

For theatre roles, there are sometimes training camps in which they train children for a particular role. Being in this training camp does not guarantee a part. It can sometimes be a big pill to swallow if your child is part of a training program for a long time (some of these programs last for a year) and then they do not get the role. I suggest to clients that while it's important for your child to want the role, they should see the training as complementary training of the highest regard. It's a great opportunity to get feedback from top professionals and whatever the outcome improvement is inevitable.

There is great magic in rejection. Your child will learn a great and very valuable life lesson early on in life. As a great song by The Rolling Stones states, 'you can't always get what you want.' Just because they may really want the job doesn't mean they will get it. They will learn the skill of caring enough to try their best but quickly moving on and learning from experiences if things do not go their way. Been as I'm on a roll here with the tunes… ' if at first you don't succeed, dust yourself off and try again' …(if you are an Aaliyah fan I bet you sang that instead of reading it) the kids who are most successful are not phased by rejection, they get back up time after time and try again approaching each audition as a new opportunity.

Your child will face rejection later in life whether or not they choose to stick within the performing arts industry. Professional rejection at interviews or personal rejections in relationships. Rejection is an inevitable part of life. Being able to manage it now will set them up for life. I find that children who have auditioned from a young age and faced disappointment develop a can-do attitude and do not take rejection so personally. They come to realise that sometimes for whatever reason their face may not fit which is nothing necessarily to do with them.

The support that you as a parent offer after a No is the biggest indicator as to whether your child will be able to cope with the industry going forward. It is important for you as a parent to get feedback if it is available. That way your child can work with their agent or performing arts teacher on those things in the hope of improving next time. If there is no feedback, then as a parent, the best thing to do is to try not to dwell. Whilst your child may be disappointed, an 'oh well' attitude where you quickly move on will serve them better than labouring what has happened.

Your child needs to know you have their back no matter what. You need to recognise where there is room for improvement, but your child still needs to know that you believe in them wholeheartedly. Easy on the first audition but not on the twenty-seventh. Always congratulate your child on trying their best, motivate your child to try again and share appropriate feedback. Remember you can help and support your child through the process, but you cannot do it for them. As a parent, you need to be the balance. The biggest fan who encourages improvement but who is satisfied that your child has tried their best. I have never known a child to thrive under parental pressure. Don't be a pushy parent. Successful kids learn, develop and excel at their own rate.

Occasionally, you will find that your child is attending the same audition as a friend or family member. You will also meet people along the way and see them at auditions. It's lovely for you and your child to make friends along the way, but it is important to remember why you are at the casting. Essentially, you are there for your child to have a shot at obtaining the job. With that said, it will sometimes be the case that your friends or people get the role and your child does not. It is important that you do not compare your child to anyone else. They need to know that they are talented and special in their own right and perhaps this time the job just was not for them.

It is also important to show good 'performance-man/woman ship,' and although they may be disappointed, they should congratulate their friend and genuinely be happy for them. (Think Oscars - when actors do not win they feel disappointed, but they still act graciously). This can be especially difficult when one sibling gets a job over another. I once had clients who were sisters. One sister used to be successful at auditions all the time and the other, although she auditioned frequently, hardly got jobs. She was always super supportive of her sister and then one day, she landed a huge role, and her sister did not know how to handle it. The other sister cried, and their mother said she compared herself to her for weeks.

It really changed the dynamics of their relationship, and that's a great shame. It became a constant comparison for everything they did going forward. As a parent, it is best for you to encourage congratulations over comparison. Also as a parent, you should not compare your children to each other or compare them to anyone else. It may not always be obvious why someone got the job over your child, so it's important that whilst they may feel disappointed they are not envious of the person who did get the job.

Going Through Changes

We are living in times where it is possible to see every race, religion, sexuality, and more recently,

disability represented on our screens and in fashion. We still have a very long way to go for it to be equal and 'the norm,' however, times are definitely changing which means that brands will want to work with a variety of different children regardless of size or colour. That's great news for children who want to make it in entertainment as it is no longer the 'traditionally pretty children' who are gaining all the work.

We are still very behind in theatre; those roles are much more race dependent. They are hardly ever advertised that way, but in the UK for sure it's nearly always the case. Simba in the Lion King is a black child, Charlie in Charlie and the Chocolate Factory is a white child. I once had a client audition for a role and not want to go to the call back because he said that it was a waste of time because the part wasn't for people of his skin colour. He was only eight at the time and very talented, so that kind of broke my heart that thought that way at such a young age, even though deep down he was right.

The USA is a bit further along than us in theatre casting 'colour blind' for some lead roles, which is refreshing but note that it may be a conversation you need to have with your child. In TV and film, it's a little more obvious and relies on storyline and casting. If they have already cast white parents and the family is a white family, it would not make sense to cast an Asian child and vice versa. Your child's look will need to fit into that particular role. It is important that they understand that this may be the reason they have been unsuccessful at times. There is a role for everyone. It is important that they do not feel that one skin colour, hair colour or type or size is more superior than another. The role just didn't fit them.

You may find yourself at a casting where they are looking for a child of a particular ethnicity, and your child is not of that ethnicity. It is amazing that with children being born into a melting pot of cultures they can often play the role of an ethnicity different from their own. Some children have so much racial ambiguity they can play the role of up to ten different Nationalities which is great for them. Look at a former actress like Meghan Markle now the Duchess of Sussex. She is mixed race but could play a woman of a number of different Nationalities. So, if you receive a casting call to go for a job that states they are looking for a child of a specific race and your child is not of that race, this may be the reason. If you feel that you have been sent to an audition that does not suit your child, always speak to your agent. I have had clients go to auditions before where their child has a black afro, and all the other boys have straight blonde hair. Perhaps a mix-up? There is no harm in double-checking with your agent so that you do not waste your time going to an audition that is not right for your child.

With all that said, it may sometimes be necessary to temporarily alter your child's appearance for a role. The most common alteration for child roles is changing their hair. You'll need to be comfortable having your child's hair dyed or styled differently for a part on some occasions. They will always try to cast a child with the colour hair they require, but they rather cast the best child for the job and then alter their hair colour. This should never be done without parental consent. If a change is required, there would usually be a meeting with the hair stylist and head of makeup artist and yourself as the parent and the child to make sure everyone was happy before work is carried out.

Sometimes your child may even be asked to cut their hair into a certain style. I once had a client with very long hair, who had been offered a huge role, but because they refused to cut their hair, they didn't get the job. It is always worth checking what is required of your child's personal appearance before you audition to ensure you are willing to make those changes if your child is successful in obtaining the job.

The other thing to note about haircuts is your child may be cast based on their original appearance, so always check before getting a haircut or changing their hair if you have a job coming up. If your child does not have a job coming up, but you want to cut their hair different to how it is in their headshots, you must let their agent know so that she can pitch a true likeness of your child to casting directors. The same thing goes for when they lose their teeth, be sure to let your agent know.

The biggest mistake people make with their kid's hair is cutting it halfway through a job. PLEASE never alter their hair once they have started a job before asking your agent first. If it's TV or film, remember it's not filmed in sequence. So if you alter their hair, there will be no continuity in how their character looks and essentially it could cut from huge afro to shaved head, and that wouldn't look good. If your child does need to change their appearance, it is important that they realise it's for the character they are playing and not a reflection of how they are perceived to look. With that said, I have had clients who have been asked to grow their hair and they have liked it so much that they kept it. So, although there may be initial resistance, they may grow to love their new look.

For all of us, there is one thing that is certain; we all get older, every single day. For kids in the spotlight, this can sometimes be a challenge. And it's not just about getting taller. For girls approaching the teenage years, their shape begins to change, and for boys, their voice breaks. For both, the dreaded zits and outbreaks can appear. Puberty can be a tough time for any teen. At this point, the types of jobs your child starts to audition for will change, not just based on their appearance but also based on the age of the characters they are being asked to portray.

You tend to find in the acting world they are asked to deal with harder hitting issues. It is important that both you and your child are comfortable with the new type of roles they may be getting. And that if they are hard-hitting, your child gets support and the storyline, the character portrayal and how it will be executed is discussed. It is also ok to turn down parts that you and your child feel they may not cope well with emotionally. Your child is the number one priority.

It also works the other way around. Some children look small for a long time, so they continue to get roles, playing children a lot younger than they truly are. This means they will have more longevity in the industry. However, teens can sometimes become more self-conscious about playing a role a lot younger than themselves. Peer pressure kicks in too. The best thing you can do to support your child through this time is to listen to them and ensure they are entirely sure of the opportunities being presented to them before they turn anything down.

It is particularly hard for boys when their voices break as it's such a noticeable change and means they no longer sound like a child. I have a client who has been in three consecutive West End shows in London. So essentially, he grew up in the theatre and then one day, his voice broke and it was in the middle of a contract, but he was replaced a few days later. He then could not have any more child roles in theatre which was hard for him to deal with. He went from performing in three shows a week and rehearsals to nothing at all. It was life-changing, but all part of growing up I guess. He soon adjusted and although not as plentiful he started doing more TV work instead.

When your child gets to what I call the 'transitional age' around 14, it can sometimes be a bit trickier for them to get work. Notoriously, over 16-year-olds are used to play teen roles as it's an easier process. No license is required, and they can work longer hours. So, don't be alarmed if you have a 14 or 15-year-old who is all of a sudden getting fewer opportunities. Have a chat with your agent and see how they can support you through this time. Maybe look at some different types of work? It is not unheard of for children to have a break from auditioning around this time to concentrate on academic studies. While this is not the right decision for everyone, it is a good time to take a break while a child is growing into a young adult.

> *"If your Mum tells you to tidy your room, don't pull out your pirate attitude. But, if someone tells you that you are not good enough, pull out your eye patch and take to the high seas."*
> *- Lindsey Sterling*

CHAPTER 8

EVEN SUPERSTARS NEED TO TIDY THEIR ROOM

No matter how famous your child becomes, they will always be your child. They will always need you and your guidance, and it is important that you know how best to support them on their journey to stardom. I guess that's why you are reading this book in the first place. The more successful they get, the easier it is to get caught up in a life of press nights, parties, and TV appearances but it's your job to keep them grounded and humble. A challenge should you choose to accept.

As a mother myself now, one thing I know for sure is that there are several different approaches to parenting. Different parents do things in different ways. There is no right or wrong approach. When your child is in the spotlight, it can sometimes mean a shift in the way that you parent to enable your child to not miss out on all the amazing things that childhood brings. You need to make decisions that other parents perhaps don't need to make and being in entertainment as a child can bring a sense of responsibility and a level of maturity far older than the age of your child.

Not to mention those teens who become social media sensations overnight and leave parents having to navigate their way through brand partnership proposals and fans wanting selfies on trips to the supermarket. There is no rule book, but it is important that parents understand as much as they can about the industry and the job they are in. Get acquainted with everyone in their world, chaperones, producers, and cast members.

You also need to be aware of any documents they are signing or deals they are making. Unfortunately, there are people out there who will prey on the vulnerability and naivety of kids, getting them to promote brands in their videos on YouTube or across other social media platforms for a nominal fee. Be sure that your child shows you emails and messages sent to them as DMs that are propositions. Ensure that your child shares everything with you. Check in on their social media daily and be sure to see what they are up to. Advise that 'fan mail' is sent to their agent and get your child's agent to check over every proposition that comes in.

You might consider using a rule app that automatically copies any emails and messages your kids receive on social media to an address, or social media account that you choose so you can monitor what your kids are doing. This could also help with child predators who target kids who want to be models and ask them to send inappropriate pics under the guise of being a modelling scout.

It's the emotional element of parenting that can be hard when parenting a child in the spotlight. Everyone is telling them how great they are, they are earning money and living a lifestyle different from their friends. It is important that they do not get caught up in the crazy world of showbiz. It can sometimes be fickle and will disappear when they stop getting work. Encourage them to still do housework, help with siblings and tidy their room at every opportunity. It is important that they still have a sense of normality in their lives. They, of course, need your encouragement and love but your job is to keep them with two feet firmly on the ground. They will thank you for it later on in life.

The spotlight can bring a lot of pressure on a kid. Peer pressure can come from school friends and friends they have made on set. Long filming or performing hours eventually take their toll. It is important that you encourage your child to talk about how they feel. If they are tired, they need to know it's fine to take a break and not to be afraid to ask for breaks. I don't mean stopping for a cup of tea and a chocolate biscuit every five minutes. But if they are in theatre and it's been a particularly busy week, it's fine for your agent to have a conversation with the producer and ask for a night off. Children need breaks every now and again, as long as it's a genuine need and not something that is requested regularly. If your child is feeling poorly, it's better to take one night off and rest than to be off for three weeks because they overdid it.

Parents of working kids have got to become particularly good at listening. Listen to everything your child tells you in great detail. If something doesn't sound right, go with your gut and ask further questions. Through listening to comments that sound completely innocent, you may be able to uncover a bigger problem or concern. Encourage your child to tell you everything. If there is an instance where they tell you something that is happening in rehearsals or on set that they are unhappy about, speak to your agent and they should help to get it sorted. Remember that kids will be kids and sometimes it's just a case of childhood bickering or an argument and they will be best friends by tomorrow. If it's an incident with an adult, try to ascertain all of the facts and have your agent approach in a professional manner. Your child's happiness and wellbeing come above everything else. Communication is key and will help to iron out any issues.

Keep a diary of everything your child tells you too. Even with all the will in the world, you'll forget. If you write things down, should you need to refer back to anything, everything will be there. You may just want to keep a diary of every time you speak to them if they are on tour. Keep track of the little details like what they ate, where they went, and what they did. Wouldn't it be a lovely thing to look back on in years to come if nothing else? It doesn't have to be a 'War and Peace' novel, just a quick note in your phone is sufficient. Kids forget stuff, some stuff is relevant, and some stuff isn't. This way, you will have it all down on paper and can refer to it. I know of a boy who made an allegation against an actor on set, through diary keeping and cross-checking his story it became apparent that he was making the story up to get attention because he felt disconnected from his friends and family. It was that diary that sorted the problem in the end. This could also work if your child were victims of bullying as you start to see patterns emerge when you record stuff.. If you suspect this, it's best to say something even if it turns out to be nothing.

Parenting is the hardest job in the world as it is, add in the mix everyone and his wife telling your child how great he or she is can be ten times harder. Kids sometimes tend to listen to other people more than they listen to their parents. They may start to 'believe the hype' and think they are too big to listen to you and to partake in household chores. Your job will be to feed them the truth and keep them grounded; to ensure they still help with household chores and respect their family and their home. If a child has been away on a tour listening to people tell them how great they are on a daily basis, it won't make sweet music to their ears. There will be times when your child will need your ultimate love and encouragement; when they approach those teen years, are changing looks, or when work is drying up. Sometimes, no matter how old we are, we all need a hug from our parents. But it can be easy to give in to your child and love in the wrong way at times because there will be times along the journey where a good kick up the bottom is needed along with encouragement. They will need to be told they can do better when deep down they know they can.

Of course, we don't want them over analysing and running themselves into the ground. But you need to be there with the encouragement when needed, and not joining the crew who's telling them how fab they are regardless of if that's true or not.

"We have to teach our kids that they can reach as high as humanly possible." - Beyoncé

CONCLUSION

So there you have it, lots to think about. A whistle-stop tour and an insight into the crazy but amazing world of showbiz. From agents to scams, to getting that first job, to rejection, we've covered it all. Being involved in showbiz as a child can be an extremely rewarding experience for you and your child. They can make some money and have a lot of fun too! They build experience that they can use throughout their lives regardless of the profession they choose. They often form lifelong friendships and sometimes, so do you as parents, especially if your child works in theatre.

Never forget why you are doing it. Make sure that enjoyment is at the heart of everything they do. Like everything in life, there are pros and cons. It's hard work. The kids face rejection, and there is lots of running around to be done but if you've got what it takes, and your child enjoys it, encourage them to reach for the stars and enjoy the ride.

Dear Mum or Dad of a future star

Thank you so much for reading my book. I really hope it's helped you along your child's journey into show business.

I'd love to hear about what you found most useful and what you plan to implement in order to help and support your child. Drop me a line to jessica@jessicaelliottmanagement.com and check out my website www.jessicaelliottmanagement.com

Can't wait for you to get in touch!

I'd also encourage you to join the Facebook group: So You Think Your Kids' Got Talent. It's a community of parents just like you and is packed full of tips, debates and advice about the industry.

Finally if you can spare a moment or two please leave me a review on the retailers website where you purchased your book to help spread the word about my book and help many more future superstars just like yours all around the world!

Here's to your success

Jx

About the Author

Jessica Elliott is a British award-winning talent agent who represents some of the most talented children in the United Kingdom. She is also the founder of a successful dance school franchise in London.

Having danced since the age of three Jessica has always had a love of performing and now dedicates her time to the success of kids in show business. Having successfully placed kids in some of the world's biggest musicals including Disney's Lion King and Matilda, provided talent for some of today's biggest stars and provided talent to the likes of Reebok, the BBC and apple to name a few it is safe to say that Jessica knows a thing or two about show business and is eager to share her knowledge and support parents.

Her free Facebook group So You Think Your Kid's Got Talent provides a wealth of support to parents and her online auditioning programs and courses prove successful with children and parents worldwide.

Aside from what goes on in front of the camera or on the stage Jessica offers support in administration, chaperoning and the safeguarding aspects of performing. Her experience has allowed her to create a unique role for herself consulting for brands and production companies when their projects involve children to ensure they are meeting all legal standards and requirements. Her influence in the industry is broad reaching and her work has lead to a number of prestigious awards.

Jessica lives in London with her husband and baby daughter who she sights as her biggest inspiration.

Printed in Great Britain
by Amazon